How to Write a Memoir in 30 Days

Step-by-Step Instructions for Creating and Publishing Your Personal Story

Roberta Temes, PhD

Reader's
digest

The Reader's Digest Association, Inc.
New York, NY • Montreal

Library of Congress Cataloging-in-Publication Data
Temes, Roberta.
  How to write a memoir in 30 days : step-by-step instructions for creating and publishing your personal story / Roberta Temes, PhD.
       pages cm.
  Summary: "A quick, fun and easy guide to writing a personal memoir in just one month. How to Write Your Memoir in 30 Days provides the framework for writers enthusiastic about telling their story, but wondering how to begin. Step-by-step techniques, culled from writers' workshops taught by the author, are presented in a welcoming, non-intimidating style. The prospect of writing a book is not daunting when compartmentalized into thirty discrete assignments"-- Provided by publisher.
  ISBN 978-1-62145-145-7 (pbk.) -- ISBN 978-1-62145-152-5 (epub)
  1. Autobiography--Authorship. 2. Report writing--Self-instruction. I. Title. II. Title: How to write a memoir in thirty days. III. Title: Step-by-step instructions for creating and publishing your personal story.
  PN147.T34 2014
  808.06'692--dc23
                              2013046368

ISBN 978-1-62145-145-7

We are committed to both the quality of our products and the service we provide to our customers. We value your comments, so please feel free to contact us.

        The Reader's Digest Association, Inc.
        Adult Trade Publishing
        44 South Broadway
        White Plains, NY 10601

For more Reader's Digest products and information, visit our website:
        www.rd.com (in the United States)
        www.readersdigest.ca (in Canada)

Printed in the United States of America

1 3 5 7 9 10 8 6 4 2

This book is dedicated to every woman and every man
who is brave enough to write the truth.
And to Judy Boros Temes, the first in my family to do so.

Acknowledgments

I am grateful to Janet Rosen, my enthusiastic, hard-working literary agent at the Sheree Bykofsky Agency, Inc. and to Andrea Au Levitt, Senior Editor at Reader's Digest, whose competence is evident throughout this book. Sincerest thanks to both of you.

Introduction

The book that's been rattling around in your head is ready to reveal itself.

Follow the daily directions within these pages and by next month you will have a memoir ready to submit for publishing.

Just write what you are asked to write for each day's assignment and your memoir will appear. You might decide to do this entirely on your computer, or you might print it out and keep your pages in a folder or you might handwrite it all in a notebook. If you prefer not to write, then speak into a recorder (perhaps your phone can record?) and when you complete the 30 assignments you will have an audio book. If you then wish to turn it into a written book, all you need to do is find a transcriptionist who will type out your recorded words.

Congratulations for undertaking this project. Your memoir will let the world know just who you are and what you've been through all these years. Whether you're writing so that colleagues will know your professional story, or so that relatives will know the truth about your family story, your memoir is important. They may not yet realize it, but your children and their children and grandchildren may one day want to know about you—your opinions, your ideas. The general public may appreciate your story, too. An interesting story is worth telling. It is wise to leave a written or oral legacy. Learning about your life—your milestones as well as your struggles—is instructive and useful, and it can be entertaining, too. All your readers can learn from you—they can learn about hopes and about happiness, and perhaps unhappiness, too. How did you do it? How did you get this far? You can be an inspiration, or a warning, depending upon your life story.

Tell them. Teach them. What were the major conflicts of your life? How did you resolve those conflicts? Do you still resolve conflicts that way? Were the conflicts with other people? Were the conflicts within yourself? The writing assignments you do will clarify all these situations.

As you delve into your past, you will notice certain themes and patterns that continue to show up in your life. Recalling some old, formerly forgotten memories will help you make sense out of your life and increase your understanding of yourself. You will give a voice to your desires, disappointments, and accomplishments, too.

Releasing repressed emotions helps you mature emotionally; often when you write about past events, buried emotions come into your mind. Writing your memoir has some neurological value, too. It stimulates your memory and thus increases your cognitive functioning. Studies have shown that when people write about personal thoughts for as few as ten minutes each day, they have an easier time falling asleep and staying asleep throughout the night. Writing about negative life events frees your mind from secretly storing those memories and you will notice that you'll have more available energy. When your writing allows you to reexperience positive life events, you boost your happiness level. When you let your true self be known, you invite others to appreciate you.

Memoirs fall into different categories. Perhaps you already know in which category your memoir belongs. It might be:

- **A relationship memoir:** Relationship memoirs show the reader how your relationship with one particular person changes over time and how you change because of that relationship. Often the relationship is a parent, a sibling, or a teacher.

- **An animal memoir:** Animals, especially household pets, play important roles, teach lessons, give love, and often provide deep and meaningful relationships.

- **An illness memoir:** Narratives about disease and illness may end in courage and triumph, or may end in tragedy. Readers stay with you throughout your ordeal. You may be the patient or you may be the caregiver.

- **A religious memoir:** Whether your faith is lost or your faith is found, your experiences resonate with readers who have had similar struggles and perplexing questions.

- **A business memoir:** A memoir about your world of work can be inspiring, specifically when you recount your failures as well as successes.

- **A travel memoir:** Your trip is both a travelogue of fascination and an inner journey showing the readers how the trip changed you.

- **A romantic memoir:** Romance in all its forms attracts readers who hope you make good choices and worry about you when you don't. In this category are memoirs about marriage, divorce, far-flung lovers, and second-time-around couples.

- **A tell-all memoir:** Secrets are revealed and a part of your past that most people never suspected is described, dissected, and discussed.

- **A disaster memoir:** Your experience surviving a burglary, a kidnapping, an earthquake, or any other disasters are included in this category.

- **A coming-of-age memoir:** The child or adolescent learns how to navigate through the adult world, with all its complicated rules and regulations.

- **A call-to-action memoir:** Readers are encouraged to become part of a social action group that will try to change a particular policy.

Your memoir may overlap several of the memoir categories or it may defy all attempts at classification and maintain a unique status. Categorizing your memoir can help you focus your writing on the themes you most want to cover. And, if you want to sell your memoir to a publisher, it gives you an easy way to describe your work. If you want to be impressive, you can refer to your writing as a literary memoir or as a personal nonfiction narrative.

After you complete each daily assignment simply save it. Later on, you'll be instructed in techniques that will merge all your daily writings into one memoir. If you wish to include material from a blog or personal journal, that, too, will be merged.

You are in charge of figuring out how quickly you complete your memoir. I hope you will find time to write every day; that maintains your momentum and you truly will finish in one month. Some people set their alarm for one hour earlier than usual and write every morning, and then finish the assignment at the end of the day. Of course if you are able to work on your memoir only on the weekends, or perhaps only three days a week, the program will still work for you. No matter how you choose to do this, you will have a completed memoir at the end of 30 writing sessions.

Many writers prefer a specific writing place—a desk in the bedroom, a particular table at the local coffee shop, or a special chair in the living room. A designated writing area is a good idea because your brain will immediately associate your writing spot with actual writing, and extraneous thoughts will stay away. You won't be tempted to think of other things when you sit down to write.

Please write about yourself with enthusiasm and with honor. Your memoir is a story and you are the main character—you are the hero. In a literary work, the main character is referred to as the protagonist. This is your life and you are in charge of how you present it.

Day 1

Think about your life and then sum it up in two or three sentences. Don't rush; let your mind wander in all directions. You may focus on particular years or precise points of your life, or you may choose to encompass a wide range of experiences.

Here are some examples of two- and three-sentence summaries:

I was blessed with good genes. I've had good luck. There are no regrets.

Pathetic life. My dog is my best friend.

Please don't be scared of me. I have schizophrenia. I would never hurt anyone.

I'm lucky because I always sleep well. But I've been unlucky because I never work well. I've had lots of job problems.

My uncle ruined my life. He molested me not once, but twice. And I let him.

I definitely married the wrong man. I have great kids. He doesn't see them, thank God.

My son wants to kill me. This is the truth.

I sell real estate. It is a big bore. I know I should look for a new job, but I can't get started.

My whole life I have messed up. My whole life she has gotten me out of messes. I wonder every day if I could change.

My mom was always sick. My dad bolted. My childhood was lousy.

Dance, aerobics, tennis, and yoga. That's my life.

People don't know that I am lonely and sad. That's because I am rich and handsome. People are easily fooled.

I have one wife and two kids. No brothers or sisters. One cousin and that's it, my entire universe.

I'm sick and tired of gambling. But I don't stop. I tried medication and I've had all kinds of therapy but nothing worked.

I love to read. I love to work. Life is great.

My childhood was traumatic. My teen years were terrible. Finally, I am happy now.

Religion saved me and now I want to spread the word. Before my awakening, I was nasty.

I used to drink. My husband divorced me. Now I am clean and sober.

I'm lonely. But maybe it's my fault because I don't like anybody.

I am obedient to a fault. Have always been like that.

Life was hard for my parents but easy for me. Good education, good jobs, great family. I am blessed.

I was once a bad boy. Lots of trouble. But I'm doing good in the world today. (This is written by Murray, who will share his writing with you as he follows the daily assignments.)

I struggled when we came to America. It was worth it. I have a fabulous husband and a kid to be proud of. (This is written by Judy, who will share her writing with you as she follows the daily assignments.)

Now it's your turn. You might write and rewrite; that's okay. Think about your life and permit all your memories to rise up in your mind. Pondering to produce your sentences stimulates your memory and makes it easier for you to recall your early years and the significant events of your life.

Day 2

A memoir is not an autobiography. An autobiography is strictly factual and chronologically covers your life from birth until today. It is accurate and full of facts and explanations. An autobiography states facts, whereas a memoir describes your reactions to those facts. For example, an autobiography might discuss social and political ideas of the times, but your memoir would discuss your emotional responses to those ideas. Your autobiography is a photograph, a picture showing precise detail. Your memoir, on the other hand, is an impressionistic painting—a canvas conveying a general impression using free brushstrokes to create a general feeling.

Memoirs are emotional reminiscences. Your memoir is your account of how you remember certain experiences. It's only as accurate as your memory permits and that's just fine. It's more important that you accurately portray your emotions than accurately list the facts. It's okay to approximate dialogue and it's okay to present events out of order. It is not okay to create imaginary events and imaginary characters, but enhancing what already exists is occasionally appropriate.

In your memoir, you will talk about and describe certain memories, figuring out why they are important. You'll investigate how and why particular incidents influenced your life.

Don't give in to the temptation to simply present your life, one year at a time, as an autobiographical report. Your memoir will cover only a few select years, or only a few select issues. Sometimes a memoir discusses only one aspect of your life, and sometimes a memoir is about a consistent theme that runs throughout your life.

There are memoirs about high school years, about years devoted to bringing up babies, about years of caring for a sick relative. There are memoirs about a lifelong relationship with a beloved teacher, with a mentally ill parent, with a family pet. You might write a memoir about your trip to France or about your search for a long-lost relative or about your years as a victim of a rare disease. None of these are autobiographical summaries of your life starting at birth; rather they are memoirs about specific time periods or specific situations.

As you write your memoir, you may discover what really happened. You may uncover a secret or two. Readers will recognize themselves in your life. Usually, your memoir reveals a universal truth. For example, Supreme Court Justice Sonia Sotomayor's memoir, *My Beloved World*, shows the reader that Sotomayor, in true immigrant fashion, began her American life in a public housing project. She recounts that upon being diagnosed with diabetes as a child, she realized she could not depend upon anyone else, but had to learn to take care of herself and her health needs. That is a defining moment for readers who will remember when they figured out that they, too, must be strong for themselves, when there was no one on whom to depend.

Similarly, in *An Unquiet Mind*, Kay Redfield Jamison, a distinguished psychiatrist, honestly recounts her own bouts with mental illness, and readers learn that knowing about disease does not provide immunity. Starkly describing her violent escapades and suicide attempts, as well as her manic episodes, Jamison gives the reader permission to admit terrors that they, too, may have experienced because of a brain gone out of control through no fault of their own. Your secrets, your flaws, and surrounding dysfunctions and misconceptions will endear your reader to you. As you explore and explain your imperfections, you create a compelling emotional journey.

Today's assignment is to look at the following list of words and write one or two sentences about each. Write whatever thoughts, memories, and ideas come into your mind. This list is meant to evoke emotional memories. Please do not reread what you have written until you are finished with the entire list.

- Disappointments

- Accomplishments

- Conflicts

- Fears

- Luck (or lack, thereof)

- Enemies

- Gratitude

Now choose whichever topics seem most relevant to you and your life. There's no need to write about a topic that has little meaning to you. The list above may have just a few topics that resonate with you. That's fine. Simply write a few paragraphs, or more if you wish, expanding your thoughts. If you see a connection between today's writing and yesterday's summary of your life, please indicate what that connection is.

Sample

I was criticized a lot when I was a kid. Not only by my mother and my grandmother, but also by the very strict teachers at parochial school. Any little mistake got a punishment. Eventually, I figured out that if I did nothing and never tried I wouldn't get in trouble for making a mistake. That's when I shut up and did not speak in class. So today I'm a grown-up and I don't really know how to participate in life.

This sample is from the writer who on Day 1 wrote, *I'm lonely. But maybe it's my fault because I don't like anybody.* She selected "fear" as her topic today, describing how her fear of making a mistake prevents her from socializing, and how her fear of being criticized prevents her from speaking when in a group.

Sample

I was a disappointment from the day I was born. Mom told me so many times that she was hoping for a girl and, at first, she didn't believe the doctor when she said it was another boy. I continued to disappoint my mother by not being as good a student as my big brothers and not being as good-looking, either. She would never admit that my looks were not up to par. She would just say, "Don't worry, you will grow into your nose." And now that Mom is in Senior House do you think my brothers, the favorites, the ones who were accepted for who they were, are looking after her? No way. It's all on my shoulders. I go to Senior House every Wednesday after work and all day on Saturdays.

This is the beginning of a memoir about the author's relationship with his mother during her final years. Those years give him his first opportunity to have long talks with her, and his readers are privy to those conversations.

You might decide to write about disappointments you have experienced at certain times. Writing about those experiences actually diminishes their effect on you. So, by writing, for example, about feeling disappointed when you were not selected for a particular promotion, you actually dilute those strong feelings that your mind originally associated with your not getting what you wanted. The more you examine the details of the situation, from all viewpoints, the less the situation will bother you.

Sample

Accomplishments were not important to my parents. Unlike most working-class Italian parents mine were not interested in accumulating money or buying a house or having a child who would be outstanding in school or in sports. Instead my parents cared only about religion. Their best accomplishment was prayer. In my mind I can still hear them,

"Mario, hurry up so you have time to pray before you get too sleepy."

"Mario, be sure you go to church in the morning."

"Mario, thank the Lord for getting rid of that bad cough you had."

When I think about it now it's a wonder I ever succeeded in school or at work. Hmm. Maybe the Lord was at work.

This author writes about his lifetime relationship with Catholicism—loving it, hating it, hiding from it, trying to change it, ignoring it, embracing it, and studying it as an academic.

Sample

Why is it that my children got along well with all their grandparents but not so much with me and my husband? Generational conflicts are repeating themselves and now we get along with our grandchildren better than they get along with their parents. The grandkids call us and email us and share their news with us and we are happy to listen to them and go places with them. Last summer, we took them on a fabulous trip. I think my daughter might have been jealous.

This is from a travel memoir about a European vacation with grandchildren.

Sample

I had so many fears when I was a kid, it's a wonder I ever left the house. It's a wonder that I wasn't bullied. Actually, I was bullied by my siblings but I don't think you count family bullying. I used to cry in school if an insect flew into the classroom. I used to run to the bathroom to brush my teeth after every meal, even a meal in the school cafeteria. I was afraid of tooth decay. I heard about it from a TV commercial. I was also afraid of halitosis, restless leg syndrome, and ED. The ED commercials really scared me. It wasn't until I was brave enough to ask my parents what that meant that I could breathe a sigh of relief. Girls couldn't get it.

This is part of an essay about the author's phobias. She has written a series of humorous essays, each mocking a different aspect of her childhood personality. When you read personal narratives, you will notice that many writers are self-deprecating and use humor to express serious feelings about serious situations.

Sample

> I had the good luck of being born into a family of well-known scholars. I had the bad luck of having an undiagnosed learning disability. Nonverbal learning disabilities (NVLD) are not much understood and some teachers say they don't believe they exist. If they lived with my brain for just one day, they'd change their mind.

This is a memoir of the author's efforts to publicize NVLD and get kids diagnosed at an early age and then provide the parents and schools with appropriate information for remediation. His fights with the system are documented.

Sample

> My father thought we had lots of enemies. He thought the Commies were after us. Every time I invited a friend over after school, he wanted my mom to quiz them about their loyalty to the United States. I thought my father was overreacting. Little did I know he couldn't help himself. By the time I was in fourth grade, it was not just Commies he was afraid of, it was our neighbors and the mailman and drivers in cars passing in front of our house. I learned how to live with a dad who had paranoia and was eventually diagnosed with paranoid schizophrenia. It wasn't that bad once I knew where he was coming from. I usually could calm him and if he took a nap he would be less paranoid when he woke up. He has never agreed to take any of the medication that's

been prescribed for him and he's never gotten better. But he's never gotten worse, either. At least it was never boring in my house.

This memoir is about the author's childhood and the accommodations he had to make because of his father's mental illness. The reader does not feel sorry for either the dad or the son because most of the misunderstandings are presented in a humorous fashion. This is another example of writing about a serious subject in a light way; it is a memoir-writing technique that works well.

Sample

My parents risked their lives so I could grow up in America. Gratitude comes naturally to me. They went through so much hardship. But here in suburbia, my peers get bent out of shape if they can't have the latest iPhone and I don't like to admit it but sometimes I get upset, too, about stupid materialistic stuff that I wish for.

This college student is writing a memoir to understand the cultural conflicts she experiences.

When you choose the topic(s) you'll write about, please give the reader plenty of details. Think of several examples of how that topic shaped you. Allow the topic you choose to help you decide what you want the reader to know about your life.

It's important that you write whatever is on your mind. Do not censor yourself. Do not worry about your ability as a writer. Later on, toward the end of the thirty days, you will quickly and easily learn how to polish your writing. For now, the idea is to write and write and write. Your story is original and your story is important. You are the only one who can write your memoir; many people can edit grammar and sentence structure. Do your job now and write, and then write some more. Techniques such as dialogue writing and scene setting and character development will be taken care of as you proceed through your daily assignments.

Day 3

Search your memory and write a few paragraphs about a time in your life when you were waiting. Maybe you were waiting for something to happen, maybe you were waiting for someone to appear, maybe you were waiting for your feelings to change.

If your thoughts and feelings are positive and happy, you will enhance your memories and your optimism as you recall the pleasant and cheerful aspects of your fortunate life. But, if when you were a child you thought there was no way to escape certain negative feelings, writing now about what your life was really like then, will help you understand your past. Perhaps, as you grew older, you realized that you could change your feelings by talking to others and by talking to yourself, by listening to music, by exercising, or by writing. Writing about your thoughts and feelings is a valid psychotherapeutic technique that can actually change the way you react to certain circumstances.

Sample

I can see myself leaning against the brick wall of our apartment building. Waiting. The older girls, they must be about seven or eight, are playing potsy—that's the Bronx version of hopscotch—on the sidewalk right in front of me. They throw their skate keys into each chalk-drawn box and hop around the grid they've created on the concrete. The boys, who are definitely older because they have permission to play in the gutter, are playing punch ball—that's the Bronx no-bat version of softball—with a pink Spaldeen.

You might think it's a typical 1940s spring day, but it's not typical at all. My mother declared today a special day. She's been polishing the furniture and scrubbing the lino-leum in our little apartment since dawn. While cleaning, she sings a ditty she's made up: "My husband's coming home. My husband's coming home from the war."

Waiting in front of our building, I'm broadcasting, "My mother's husband is coming home, my mother's husband is coming home from the war," to all passersby. I wonder, what would he look like—this husband?

I see a guy emerge from the Jerome Avenue subway station on the corner. He hoists a green duffel bag over his shoulder. Oh, I guess he's not my mother's husband, he walks right by me and enters our apartment building.

I'm still waiting when he returns a few minutes later with my mother. Is this my mother's husband? My father? I doubt it. I'm almost five years old and I know from the pic-ture books that Miss Marjorie reads to us in nursery school that fathers smoke pipes and wear hats and suits and ties. This guy is wearing a T-shirt and chino pants and he looks too skinny to be a father.

He abruptly lifts me, whirls me, and then says we should go inside. He and my mother hold each other's waists, then they hug, and then they each take one of my hands and together we walk into apartment 1E.

My mother's husband has come home.

In our cozy two rooms, he stares at me and tells me I was a baby when he left. I doubt that. It's been a long time since I was a baby.

Finally, I am brave enough to ask, "Are you my daddy?"

His answer still haunts me.

The above essay about waiting gives the reader much information without explicitly stating facts. The author does not say she was brought up in a city but instead takes us directly to her apartment building and a nearby subway station. At the beginning of the essay, she does not state her age, but instead mentions that she is younger than the seven- and eight-year-olds. She does not name the year but tells us about world happenings during that year. And most important, she does not tell us we will be reading a memoir about a difficult relationship between father and daughter. We surmise that and we are curious to find out what the dad said that still disturbs her. The more the reader is called upon to think, the more engaged the reader becomes with you and your memoir.

Sample

It seems like I spent my whole marriage waiting to have kids. It's all I ever wanted. I wanted to be a dad like my dad was to me. We did so much stuff together and we were a team. I could hardly wait to have a team with my kids. Rebecca said she wanted a family when we were dating, but after we got married she kept saying "Next year, next year." I was relieved when she finally said okay we could start trying, and I was disappointed every month when it turned out she wasn't pregnant. And then the truth came out.

The author gets us interested and we want to read more to find out what that truth was. When you write your sentences and paragraphs to fulfill your daily assignments, use subtlety and give hints to the reader rather than presenting all the facts.

Day 4

Thinking about your past and about the important decisions you have made in your life, please write three essays today. Each will be just one or two pages. And each will begin with one of the sentences below. Please refer back to your Day 1 life summary if you need to jog your memory.

Essay one: *In that moment I realized that . . .*

Essay two: *If only . . .*

Essay three: *It started out as an ordinary day, but then . . .*

Sample

He was the third doctor we went to. He was calm and he was thoughtful. He looked at me and Rebecca with soulful eyes. **In that moment I realized that** there was no way out. We were just beginning a long journey.

This is the beginning of a memoir of a family living with a child who has a terminal illness. Note that the author hooks us right away. There is no introduction about how old Rebecca is or what is wrong with her. We don't even know if the narrator is mother, father, spouse, or someone else. When you begin your memoir with a gripping paragraph, the reader is eager to continue reading and you then have the luxury of presenting background information at any time. Also note that the introductory phrase does not appear until sentence four and that is acceptable when the previous sentences heighten the suspense.

Sample

If only my parents had discussed marriage with me, I might not have jumped into my first marriage when I was barely 18 years old. My mother and I had a good relationship. But she didn't think it was her place to give me advice. I said I loved him and wanted to marry him, so she replied, "When?"

Neither Mom nor Dad asked if I knew anything about his family. I didn't and that's because he was estranged from them, and he was only 21. I thought it might be impolite to ask what the issues were.

My parents didn't want to pry, or so they said years later, and that's why they never asked me why he became enraged whenever I asked him to dress appropriately—wear a suit to a wedding or ironed, presentable clothes every day. I, of course, thought if I showed him sufficient love and kindness he would change after we married.

This is the beginning of an essay that the author writes about her first marriage. She goes on to write essays about two more marriages and then ends her series of several more essays with a final piece describing her satisfying relationship with her cat.

Essays can be compiled to equal one book. You might create a book consisting of many two-page essays or you might write several long pieces interspersed with shorter ones, or you might write a full-length memoir. Some writers, particularly those who are planning to present family and friends with a memoir at a significant birthday celebration, prefer a shorter book.

Sample

It started out as an ordinary day but then Marcy, my wife of three years, said she wanted to talk to me about something very important. I figured it was money. She's the one who pays the bills, handles the checkbook, and knows more about our finances than I do. I just give her my paycheck every two weeks and she adds hers to it and then goes to the bank and comes home with cash for me until the next time we get paid. It works, but sometimes she complains, so I was ready to hear her complaints.

There were no complaints.

Instead, she had on her serious face and said, "Pete, you know I love you very much, right?"

"Yeah," I said.

"You know I'd never want to hurt you, right?"

"Yeah," and now I'm wondering where this is leading.

"You never did anything wrong, Pete. It's me. I'm just not happy."

"What's wrong, Marcy? You can tell me what's bothering you. We always work things out."

"It's more than that, Pete."

"Do you want to go back to that therapist you went to when you were in college? We have good insurance."

"No, Pete. I want to leave you. I want a divorce."

The room started to spin. I felt nauseous and hoped I wouldn't throw up right there at the kitchen table. I wanted to cry. I wanted to call my mother, but she'd been dead for a couple of years already. I wanted to shake my wife. I wanted to run into bed and get under the covers. I did none of those things. I just sat there like an idiot.

Note that a dramatic incident begins the memoir and the background information is postponed until the author is certain that we are hooked.

Sample (from Murray)

In that moment I realized that I was throwing away my life. Why was I in a jail cell? Well, I knew why. And I deserved to be there. But looking around, I realized I'd soon be dead if I continued with my drug habit. I begged the judge to send me to rehab.

If only I had done this a few years earlier, I would have saved myself and my family all those years of horror. Being a drug addict is no fun. You are always suffering or making other people suffer.

It started out as an ordinary day. Just another day to look for money to feed my habit, to get wasted. But then someone called the cops. I was so mad. Now, I know it was what I needed to turn my life around.

How are you doing with your writing? Is investigating your past interesting? Scary? Fun? If you prefer writing your essays about current situations that is your prerogative—go for it. Some writers prefer concentrating on recent life events, while others find more meaning in memories from an earlier time.

Day 5

You have assumed many roles in your life. Some of the roles were given to you and others you chose.

Recall how you felt about yourself in a role you had just briefly. Even if you had a role for just a short time—perhaps you were a waitress, a wallflower, or a wanderer—during that short time your self-image was altered. Recall a role that provided you with an identity—mom? physician? neighbor?—and write about how that role helps you define yourself today.

If you are like most adults you relate to your neighbors, your coworkers, your friends, and most everyone you interact with, in a manner similar to the way you related to everyone in your family of origin while growing up. Bossy or compliant, loud or quiet, reflective or impulsive, these traits usually remain consistent throughout life.

Often the workplace replicates a family. One person in the workplace becomes the nurturer or mother figure; another becomes the authority figure, perhaps looked upon as the dad. Then there is the worker who feels entitled to more privileges than the other employees. Perhaps that worker was the spoiled kid in his family of origin. Of course, when employees vie for their supervisor's attention they are reenacting sibling rivalry.

So, think about your roles in your family, at school, at work, and elsewhere. When you write about recent incidents in your life, you may be able to connect your actions with long-ago roles.

Read through the list below, select several roles that are relevant to you, and write a paragraph or more about each. Select the roles that elicit strong feelings—positive or negative—since every role you have played has left its mark on you.

- Attention-seeker
- Babysitter
- Best friend
- Breadwinner
- Bully
- Caretaker
- Class clown
- Crybaby
- Delinquent
- Employer
- Gang member
- Healer
- Helper
- Loser
- Loudmouth
- Martyr
- Nag
- Shy one
- Spoiled brat
- Stepchild
- Stepparent
- Student
- Teacher
- Troublemaker
- Winner

The above list is not exhaustive. Please feel free to write about a role not listed here, as well. You are encouraged, of course, to write about your role as parent, sibling, and/or child within your family.

Write about as many of the roles above as you wish, then answer any or all of these questions, using details and descriptions:

- What roles were you expected to play when you were young? Which roles do you now play?

- Is there one role that is/was most satisfying? Why?

- Is there a role that is/was very disappointing or difficult? Why?

- Is there a role you wish you could play out differently if you had the opportunity to redo your actions? What changes would you make?

- Is there a role you are still yearning to play?

Sample

I loved being a babysitter when I was a teenager. It was the only opportunity I had to be alone. The baby would be asleep upstairs and I'd be downstairs in the spacious living room of our across-the-street neighbors' house. In my house, there was no spacious living room. My grandma lived with us and the living room was actually used as her bedroom. And our house was always full of people—relatives from out of town, my father's brother who stopped in to chat, friends of my mom who wanted to enjoy her homemade apple pie, and my brother and two sisters and their friends. So, babysitting was like heaven to me. Quiet, no drama, just one sleeping babe. I used those hours to read and to think. And I did have a lot to think about.

And now the writer can segue into memories and thoughts that reveal her inner life. She's prepared the reader by announcing that she enjoyed time alone to think. She didn't use that time to chat with friends, to experiment with makeup, to watch television, to listen to music. No, instead she used that time to think. What thoughts were so compelling?

Sample

I wished for a best friend throughout elementary school. Finally, when I was in eighth grade I found one. But it wasn't the kind of friend you might expect. People did call me weird and sometimes called me crazy, but I loved my best friend. His name was Silly and he was a ferret.

From the day I got Silly, I never again felt lonely and I never again thought about running away. I knew that he loved me and he needed me. He was very playful and ran around my basement, where I kept him, all the time. He was smart and could learn where I wanted him to stay and what parts of the house were off-limits.

I actually lost weight during my years with my best friend because he was so active and I was always chasing him. I could tell that Silly loved me as much as I loved him. Silly was actually good practice for me. After he died and I got over his death, I was ready to look for a human companion. I did and that's how I met my girlfriend.

The writer used this as the beginning of his coming-of-age story. A coming-of-age story is one in which the writer shows how he made the transition from childhood to adolescence to adulthood. Self-discovery and loss of innocence are the usual themes.

Sample

School was a good place for me. I never had to try hard. Learning the lessons was easy. Making friends, not so easy.

I wished the teachers would be my friends, even when I was in the lower grades. They were so logical and tame. The kids were unpredictable and wild and, in hindsight, childish. That's when I started thinking about becoming a teacher. And today I am a teacher. I help the kids who are like I was—shy, smart, nerdy, and socially uncomfortable.

The author's memoir is an account of her many years as a teacher in a suburban school system.

Sample

I wanted to be a dad more than anything in the world, so I was thrilled to meet Teena who had a little boy and no husband. I think I wanted to be a dad because I wanted to show the world that I could be a good one, as good as my own, maybe even better. But it didn't work out that way because little Tim always felt guilty if he was nice to me. He felt like he was betraying his real father so he never let me be a true stepfather to him. It was disappointing to me and eventually I realized that Teena was not the love of my life because it was Tim—and the idea of being a step-father—that pulled me to her. I got over my desire to be the world's greatest dad when I thought a lot about my childhood and remembered that my dad made mistakes along the way. So, I didn't have to prove I was perfect and I waited until I met the right woman to marry. Clare and I have been married for eighteen years and have two kids. I am a good father and try my best to be patient. It gives me satisfaction when I remember times that my own dad blew his top when we were misbehaving.

This memoir is about the writer's relationship with his father with emphasis on his father's final years in a nursing home.

Sample

I wish I could be a mom again to my children when they were young. I was so caught up in rebelling against my own mother's way of doing things that I often went to extremes with my kids and was not the best mother. My mother insisted upon a rigidly fixed bedtime, so I let my kids stay up as late as they wanted. My mother gave us a lot of chores to do, so my kids had no responsibilities in the house.

This writer's story is about her years looking for her runaway daughter.

Day 6

Your memoir will focus on what you did to accomplish a particular mission or to reach a specific point in your life. How you got there is the prominent story within your memoir. These actions are your plot. Your memoir is actually a detailed emotional account of your pursuit to fulfill your mission. Today's assignment is to think long and hard and figure out what mission you want to write about. What is the point of your memoir?

When you can state this mission in one sentence you have truly begun writing your memoir. Then, you'll be ready to write about the people involved in this plot, the setting in which this story takes place, and the actions you took to fulfill your mission.

For today's assignment, please complete this sentence; it is your mission statement:

My memoir describes what I went through in order to _____

_____.

George Orwell stated, "When I sit down to write a book . . . I write it because there is some lie that I want to expose." You may have different motivation. Your mission need not be horrifying and it need not be an exposé. It can be what you went through in order to have a lovely family, and you can write about choices and decisions you made along the way to reach that goal. Your mission might be what you went through in order to overcome a serious disability or how you became the successful person you are today.

It's possible that coming up with your mission statement may bring to mind some difficult times and risky situations that you downplayed while you focused on achieving your goal. Now, in retrospect, you can give yourself permission to feel the emotions you were withholding. It is a mark of maturity to withhold emotions while going through a crisis. It is also a mark of maturity to finally recognize those emotions, if they become evident when the crisis is over.

Psychologists define repression as the process of keeping away some unpleasant thoughts and not permitting anxiety-producing memories to intrude upon daily life. Sigmund Freud, the founder of psychoanalysis, believed that repression was a bad trait and that talking about unpleasant issues was necessary for a good life. That's no longer considered true. Research shows that some people are better off simply forgetting about their traumas.

The beauty of memoir writing is that your memory will permit you to remember only those incidents that are good for you to remember. Repression will kick in and prevent you from recalling memories that may be too disturbing. If you can handle it, it will appear; if it doesn't appear when you ask yourself to recall it, then this is not the time for it to surface. That's why some people who were sexually abused often don't recall the memory until decades later. Life presents many tragedies and many traumas and we all find our way of coping. Some deny, some distract, some delve right in. Your way is right for you.

Sometimes, after the passage of time, a painful memory may intrude upon your consciousness. If this happens to you, then writing about it may be your best therapy. Writing is an intelligent method of helping you understand your feelings about traumatic occurrences. Dark, disturbing memories diminish when they are brought out into the light.

Here's a warning: Telling the truth will help you figure out past problems. But do not assume that other family members will also benefit. Revealing secrets and forgiving past transgressions may make you feel good but will not necessarily heal all family members. Author William Zinsser said, "To defend what you have written is a sign that you are alive." So, be brave.

Samples

My memoir describes what I went through in order to . . .

- . . . make sense out of those years my mother abandoned me.
- . . . become a psychiatrist.
- . . . stay in the police department.
- . . . love my stepson.
- . . . make a new life in Florida after my wife died.
- . . . become a model even though I was not skinny.
- . . . get my father to love me.
- . . . understand my roommate's suicide.
- . . . become wealthy.
- . . . forgive my priest.
- . . . divorce my wife and marry my girlfriend.
- . . . prevent my son from finding out who his biological father is.
- . . . be compassionate to my brother who has mental illness.
- . . . buy the house of my dreams—and furnish it, too.
- . . . fight city hall.

. . . be the perfect daughter, perfect wife, and perfect mother.

. . . understand my parents' divorce.

. . . make a good life in America.

. . . raise my children as a single parent.

. . . enjoy my vacation in Vietnam.

. . . become a wise old lady.

. . . adjust to sudden poverty.

. . . make sense out of my cancer diagnosis.

Clear Communication: Spelling

The subject about which you are writing—your life—is fascinating. Now it's time to be sure that your terrific story is being told in a way that your readers can easily understand. Your writing must be clear and free of grammatical errors. So, from now on, at the end of each day's assignment you'll find some helpful information about word usage, sentence structure, spelling, or grammar. Communicating to your readers with clarity and precision is the goal.

Of course, you can ignore this last section of each day's work and just concentrate on your memories. You might decide to engage the services of a freelance editor to take care of the grammatical part of your book or you might decide to work on these items as a project after your 30 days of writing.

Today, let's talk about spelling. Correct spelling is still crucial for communication, even though when we tweet or text we abbreviate and deliberately misspell. Correctly spelling all the words in your memoir tells your readers that you have something important to say, something that cannot be tweeted. Your readers will connect with you and clearly understand you when you present proper spelling. Your ideas, no matter how profound, are easily discounted when words are misspelled.

Be certain that the spell-checker on your word-processing program is activated. Check it out by deliberately misspelling a word and then seeing if your computer catches it. As useful as a spell-check program is, however, sometimes it misleads you. If you correctly spell the wrong word, you'll never know it's the wrong word. For example, if you type *loose* instead of *lose* your computer will let it pass because *loose* is not misspelled, it's misused.

Lose, spelled with one *o,* is pronounced as if the s is a *z.* You may *lose* your keys, you may *lose* your mind, and you may *lose* a game of Words with Friends. You may *lose* a tooth, but only if that tooth is *loose. Loose,* spelled with two *o*'s, rhymes with goose.

If you confuse *lose* and *loose* you are not alone. A popular website for losing weight had to also reserve the URL for a website that promises to help people "loose weight." Yes, it's grammatically incorrect, but so many people put the term *loose weight* into a search engine that it was necessary to have such a web page.

Please use *loose* when you write about something that is free and unattached or shaky—a *loose* cannon, a *loose* shoe, a dog running *loose.* When uncertain about the spelling just say the word aloud in your sentence and if it needs a *z* sound, it is *lose.*

Back to spelling: the most often misspelled word in the English language is purported to be *separate.* Whether you are using the word to explain that you must place feuding siblings in different rooms, thereby *separating* them, or give each child a distinct, and *separate* task, the word is always spelled with two *a*'s and it contains *a rat.*

Another s word that often confuses writers is *supersede*. It ends in *sede*, not *cede*. Other words often misspelled, and here spelled correctly, are:

Believe—believe has a *lie* in it

Broccoli—two *c*'s and one *l*

Calendar—the order of the vowels is *a—e—a*

Cemetery—all *e*'s, no *a*

Conscience—this has the word *science* in it and it refers to your inner feelings that guide your behavior

Conscious—aware and alert, ready to redeem an *IOU*—those three letters are within the word

Definite—the order of the vowels is *e—i—i—e*; there is definitely not an *a* in *definite*

Embarrass—two *r*'s and two *s*'s

Occurrence—two *c*'s and two *r*'s

Referral—two *r*'s

Weather—a faulty forecast and the weather lady must *eat her* words

Whether—*Wh* as in *why*

Spelling counts. Please check any word that you suspect might be spelled incorrectly.

Day 7

Identify an important incident from your past—one that changed the course of your life and influenced the pursuit of your mission because it was so very (choose from list below):

- Beautiful

- Frightening

- Unusual

- Spiritual

Write the story of that event. Indicate how it helps you explain what you went through in order to accomplish your mission.

Sample: Beautiful

My life was all about making money. I built a terrific business that employed 38 workers. I was generous with them and they were good to me. I didn't take the time to do what my wife wanted. She wanted me to stop and go on vacations and take day trips with her. I had no time. I was working, working, working. I never cared for traveling, anyway. Finally, she left me, and my daughters took her side in the divorce. So I was all alone, working seven days a week and I was pretty happy. My bank account was growing and my reputation in the restaurant industry was terrific.

One night a lady came into my restaurant with her daughter and son. The daughter was smiling and her eyes were shining. The son had a big smile on his face. They were a beautiful family.

I had seen them before and so I asked, "Where's your dad? He's usually with you. I hope he's okay."

The mom answered, "He's working late tonight but he will soon be joining us."

And then in about 20 minutes the dad walked in and both kids raced up to hug him. When he sat down at the table, his wife kissed him. The family looked comfortable and relaxed with each other.

When I went over to greet the father, he said, "I hurried to get here. It was tough because my desk is overflowing with work but I didn't want to disappoint my family."

The four of them sitting there looked like an ad from a magazine. They were smiling at each other, talking to each other, and the scene was beautiful.

That's when I realized that I always disappointed my family. From that day on, I made up my mind to create a beautiful family even if my wife wouldn't take me back. My wife didn't take me back. But I started calling my girls, meeting them, showing them that I could show up when I said I would. I started telling them how much I love them. I went out of my way to keep all appointments that we made. In about one year, we were a beautiful family. Me and my daughters get together all the time now and I know everything about their lives and about their feelings. That original beautiful scene of a family around the table in my restaurant taught me how to be a good father.

This is the beginning of a memoir of an older man. His mission sentence is: *My memoir describes what I went through in order to become a good father.*

Sample: Frightening

It was a cold night. I was walking from the supermarket to my car in the parking lot. There were five yellow plastic bags in the shopping cart. Each bag was brimming over with food. When I got to my car there was someone sitting in it. In fact, more than one person. There were a couple of teenagers in the backseat and a tough-looking young man in the driver's seat. What were they doing? Why were they in my car? The radio was on full blast. One of them was smoking—in my car!

When I moved to this neighborhood, my father warned me about times like this. He actually bought me a gun and took me to the shooting range. I promised him that every time I went out after dark I'd have that weapon with me. So I wasn't really scared.

First I yelled, "Get out of the car." They didn't budge.

Then I threatened them, "I'm going to call the cops," I shouted. They didn't budge.

Finally, I reached into my shoulder bag and pulled out my gun. They ran out of the car in two seconds flat and I saw that they were so young. Just aimless, stupid kids who I might have killed if they didn't quickly run.

I started to shake. My legs were too wobbly to think of driving quite yet. But I was able to think about what I almost did.

The next morning, I called my congressperson to find out about gun control laws in our area. Since that night, I've been for gun control and against guns. I will admit I still have my gun.

This is the beginning of a memoir of a political activist. The author's mission sentence is: *My memoir shows how I became a militant protester.*

Sample: Unusual

The day I went to my neighbor's daughter's wedding changed my life. When the beautiful bride walked down the aisle, she was accompanied by her parents and then right behind them was Missy, her white poodle. The dog was dressed in an adorable doggie coat and she had two red bows in her fur. When I saw that, I knew that I am not crazy for loving my dog as much as I do. My friends and my family always make fun of me because I like to include Coco in activities. I was starting to think that I was weird. But when I saw that the totally unweird, beautiful, popular, charming bride included her dog in her wedding, I felt validated. I could finally accept myself because it's okay to love my dog and it's okay to take her places with me. From that day on, I felt proud of myself, not ashamed, and I started looking for other role models, other people who had ideas I liked even if they were unusual ideas.

This writer's mission statement is: *My mission is to show how I became a secure, well-adjusted adult after being a very insecure teenager and I did it without ever going to therapy.*

Sample: Spiritual

The whole extended family showed up for my father's memorial service. The funeral was the previous week and this was a luncheon where everyone could get up and talk about their memories of him. We also made a slide show. It was a rainy afternoon, so when we pulled into the parking lot I made sure my kids rolled their windows all the way up. As we entered the restaurant, my husband looked back at our minivan and said, "Pops, we all had a good time driving you around during those last few months when you couldn't drive anymore. No one has sat in your seat yet in the car or at the dining room table; maybe after today we will." And then we went in and a good time was had by all. It was not sad; there were lots of laughs.

It was still raining when we left so we all ran toward the car. To our shock, the headlights were on and all the windows were halfway opened. My husband and I looked at each other in disbelief. Nothing was stolen from the car. The kids' iPads and jackets were still in there, my phone was right where I left it, and quarters were in the change compartment. No one had a key except my husband and he hadn't touched the key. What happened? I know what happened. My dad was informing us that he knew about the service and was with us all the way. Since that day I continue to feel his presence.

This is an excerpt from a memoir about the writer's relationship with her father.

Sample: Frightening (from Judy)

> Everything I experienced during my first few months in America frightened me. I was actually very scared on the plane. I never was on a plane before and I couldn't understand any of the announcements because they were all in English. Even the food they served scared me. I had never seen a banana and there was one on my tray so I picked it up and took a bite. The peel was hard to bite through so I kept trying and finally I succeeded. It was disgusting and I was so scared that all American food would be that bad and I'd never again have a good meal.

Judy's memoir tells of her adjustment to life in America.

To access a beautiful memory you might want to look at some old photos to jog your memory. You can remember a frightening event from your past by thinking of something that recently frightened you. Once your brain recalls one event that scared you, other such events easily come to mind. Significant memories of unusual and spiritual occasions are times when you felt otherworldly or mystical, as if something was going on that you couldn't quite grasp, but you knew it felt right.

Continue mining your memory and communicating your thoughts and feelings. You're doing a good job.

Clear Communication: Its, It's

It's easy to confuse *its* and *it's* if you don't know the rules. So, please read these instructions:

The rule about *it's*: *It's* is an abbreviation of two words. When you want to write *it is* you may leave out the second *i* and replace it with an apostrophe. *It is* then becomes *it's*. *It's* can also mean *it has*.

Here are some sentences with *it's*. Read the sentences aloud and say *it is* or *it has* wherever you see the apostrophe between the *i* and the *s*.

It's *time to write today's assignment.*

The publisher thinks it's *ready to go to the printer.*

It's *a very good memoir that you have written.*

I was looking for your writing and then I remembered it's *all on the computer.*

It's *taken you a long time to write your book.*

The rule about *its*: The main rule is that it does *not* mean *it is*. If you say *it is* when you see *its*, the sentence won't make sense. It does mean that something belongs to something else. In almost every other word in the English language, belonging or possession is indicated by using an apostrophe. However, with the words *it is* that rule does not apply. Instead, *its* is written with no apostrophe.

I'm pleased to read your memoir in its *first rendition.*

Every memoir has its *own style.*

The dog wags its *tail when I read from your manuscript.*

I went to the literary agency's building but couldn't locate its *office.*

Please check your usage of *it is* and *it's* in the writing you've done so far.

Day 8

Poet Amy Lowell wrote about standards, boundaries, and expectations. She thought she might create a new pattern in her life, and not necessarily adhere to certain expectations, with the help of the man she intended to marry. But her fiancé died before their wedding, and she was left to figure out on her own how to create a new lifestyle representing her own standards, boundaries, and expectations. Patterns are recurring themes. We all have patterns that show up in our lives—often without our permission—based upon tradition and expectations.

Here is Amy Lowell's poem, "Patterns" (your assignment follows):

I walk down the garden paths,
And all the daffodils
Are blowing, and the bright blue squills.
I walk down the patterned garden paths
In my stiff, brocaded gown.
With my powdered hair and jewelled fan,
I too am a rare
Pattern. As I wander down
The garden paths.

My dress is richly figured,
And the train
Makes a pink and silver stain
On the gravel, and the thrift
Of the borders.
Just a plate of current fashion,
Tripping by in high-heeled, ribboned shoes.
Not a softness anywhere about me,
Only whale-bone and brocade.
And I sink on a seat in the shade
Of a lime tree. For my passion
Wars against the stiff brocade.
The daffodils and squills
Flutter in the breeze
As they please.
And I weep;
For the lime tree is in blossom
And one small flower has dropped upon my bosom.

And the splashing of waterdrops
In the marble fountain
Comes down the garden paths.
The dripping never stops.
Underneath my stiffened gown
Is the softness of a woman bathing in a marble basin,
A basin in the midst of hedges grown
So thick, she cannot see her lover hiding,
But she guesses he is near,
And the sliding of the water
Seems the stroking of a dear
Hand upon her.

What is Summer in a fine brocaded gown!
I should like to see it lying in a heap upon the ground.
All the pink and silver crumpled up on the ground.

I would be the pink and silver as I ran along the paths,
And he would stumble after,
Bewildered by my laughter.
I should see the sun flashing from his sword-hilt and the buckles on
his shoes.
I would choose
To lead him in a maze along the patterned paths,
A bright and laughing maze for my heavy-booted lover,
Till he caught me in the shade,
And the buttons of his waistcoat
bruised my body as he clasped me,
Aching, melting, unafraid.
With the shadows of the leaves and the sundrops,
And the plopping of the waterdrops,
All about us in the open afternoon—
I am very like to swoon
With the weight of this brocade,
For the sun sifts through the shade.

Underneath the fallen blossom
In my bosom,
Is a letter I have hid.
It was brought to me this morning by a rider from the Duke.
"Madam, we regret to inform you that Lord Hartwell
Died in action Thursday sen'night."
As I read it in the white, morning sunlight,
The letters squirmed like snakes.

"Any answer, Madam," said my footman.
"No," I told him.
"See that the messenger takes some refreshment.
No, no answer."
And I walked into the garden,
Up and down the patterned paths,
In my stiff, correct brocade.
The blue and yellow flowers stood up proudly in the sun,
Each one.
I stood upright too,
Held rigid to the pattern
By the stiffness of my gown.
Up and down I walked,
Up and down.

In a month he would have been my husband.
In a month, here, underneath this lime,
We would have broke the pattern;
He for me, and I for him,
He as Colonel, I as Lady,
On this shady seat.
He had a whim
That sunlight carried blessing.
And I answered, "It shall be as you have said."
Now he is dead.

In Summer and in Winter I shall walk
Up and down
The patterned garden paths
In my stiff, brocaded gown.

The squills and daffodils
Will give place to pillared roses, and to asters, and to snow.
I shall go
Up and down,
In my gown.
Gorgeously arrayed,
Boned and stayed.
And the softness of my body will be guarded from embrace
By each button, hook, and lace.
For the man who should loose me is dead,
Fighting with the Duke in Flanders,
In a pattern called a war.
Christ! What are patterns for?

For today's assignment, please try to identify the patterns of your life. Did you create new patterns with a partner? By yourself? In your imagination?

Were the traditional patterns—patterns established through the generations in your family—good for you to follow? Easy for you to follow? Impossible for you to follow? What were those patterns?

What were your important choices, decisions, pathways, and themes? How did they influence your quest to fulfill your mission?

As you write you will reveal yourself to your readers. Many of the choices you have made in your life, for good and for not so good, you may have made without thorough examination, but rather by simply following a set pattern.

Your personality will show itself in all your writings. Upon examination you will become aware of certain patterns that you follow, patterns that express your personality. Choices that seem almost automatic are usually based upon traditions, which are patterns that have created expectations. The essays you are writing each day will unveil similarities in the way in which you conduct your life. Maybe you will come across as a hero in most of your essays, or maybe as a victim. Perhaps you are a philosopher looking for meanings, or are you a risk taker?

As you proceed through life, your actions express the patterns you observed while growing up and then your personality modifies those patterns. Were you rebelling against them? Were you so ambitious you exceeded them? And then, of course, luck and the vagaries of life modify the plans you had and expose you to new ideas and situations. Your reader will understand you and appreciate you once you show your attitude about life. Please reveal your true self.

Sample

In my family it was assumed that after high school I would go into my father's business, just like my two older brothers did. It was also assumed I'd marry my high school girlfriend and settle in town just like my two older brothers did. But, those patterns didn't work for me. I knew I had artistic talent and my father thought I could use it to make ads and brochures for our business. That's not the pattern I wanted to follow.

I had met a girl online who also loved to paint and she wanted to meet me in person. No one in my family ever took a plane for a blind date. It was the best thing I ever did. Anita has been my wife for nine years now. We both worked at fast-food places to pay for art school and we both have had shows in galleries and sold some work. We settled in a big city. We had to because we needed top instructors and we also need to live near people who like to spend money on art for their homes. It was hard to break the patterns that were laid out for me to follow. When we see my family at Christmas and other holidays I know that I would not have been happy following the old patterns and it is awkward. They think that we think that we are better than them. That's not true at all. We just think we're different and we have a different pattern to our lives.

Sample

This may not seem like a big deal but it was because it started to separate me and my husband from his family. In his family, all boy babies are named after the grandfather. But I had a name in mind from the time I was ten years old. I always knew that if I had a boy he would be named Brad. I even had some towels embroidered with the name on them and some bibs, too—before I was pregnant. I know that seems strange but that's how important that name was to me.

When I gave birth, my husband's family was thrilled of course but then when we told them the name, they acted as if we were poison. They stopped visiting me in the hospital and they stopped buying gifts for the baby and then they stopped talking to us, just like that. My husband warned me this might happen if I stuck to Brad but I thought he was exaggerating. We broke the family pattern and we paid a price for it. In a way, it wasn't so bad because it showed my husband that he could form his own opinions. But he is sad because he doesn't have his parents in his life anymore.

Once we were on our own, we broke more patterns and we got accustomed to making our own decisions. It didn't always work out for the better. One day we went too far and we thought we knew what we were doing and instead of going to his parents for financial advice, we listened to a guy we met on the Internet. Before we knew what was happening we were swindled out of all our wedding-present money and all our savings and then the FBI came knocking on our door.

Sample

When my brother was dying, my sister and I and our husbands visited every day and helped out as much as we could. We didn't want to burden his children who had young families and new careers. I could remember my parents doing the same when their siblings were deathly ill. This was a pattern that made sense to me. But when my husband's sister was in a nursing home, her children, our niece and nephew, asked us to stay away. They said they wanted to be alone with their mom in her final weeks. We said we'd help so they could attend to their jobs and to their children but they said no. They broke the pattern and we still haven't spoken to them. Now that I've written this, I realize that it was a pattern in my family and maybe not in theirs. I wonder how we can reconnect with them.

Like poet Amy Lowell, most of us have patterns we are expected to follow. We learn about patterns from our families, our religion, our daily lives, and the people we encounter. We also learn about patterns from popular culture—movies and television portray ideas of what is acceptable and what should be avoided. Some of us follow obediently, some of us diverge, and for all of us our expectations and our ambitions influence how we respond to the opportunities we encounter.

Clear Communication: Whose and Who's

The word *whose* is used when you are indicating possession or ownership. See the sentences below:

Whose *book is that?*

Whose *turn is it to do the dishes?*

Whose *car are you taking tonight?*

There is a professor whose *students all get high marks.*

Use the word *who's* when you mean *who is* or *who has.*

In each sentence below, you can substitute *who is* or *who has* for the word *who's*. Try it.

Who's *in the living room?*

Who's *doing the dishes tonight?*

Who's *already dressed and ready to go out?*

Who's *driving tonight?*

Look through your writing to be sure you've correctly used *who's* and *whose.*

Day 9

You grew up with certain values. You've maintained some of them, eliminated others, and created new ones, too.

Here are some widespread values:

- Accumulate consumer goods; shop a lot
- Accumulate wealth; have money in the bank
- Attend classes and keep learning
- Be active in your church/synagogue/mosque
- Be aware of current events; always read newspapers
- Be charitable; help strangers
- Be independent; rely upon only yourself
- Eat only healthful foods
- Exercise every day
- Have a warm, cozy family life
- Have an open home; offer guests food and fine wines
- Have many babies

- Keep a trim, fit body
- Live in a large home with fine furnishings
- Live modestly; don't call attention to yourself
- Live near your extended family
- Marry someone who is successful or good-looking
- Participate in sports
- Pray often
- Read constantly
- Retire early
- Show off your wealth
- Take vacations as often as possible
- Travel extensively
- Trust only blood relatives
- Volunteer in your community

Identify the values you grew up with, the values you accumulated during your life, and the values you have today. Write anecdotes and memories of certain values and how they influenced your life. It's important for the reader to know about incidents that shaped you and changed you. Were those events brought about because you were attempting to maintain certain values? When you write your essays tell the reader about significant events and show the reader how you reacted to those events.

- How did you react to those events when they conflicted with your values?

- How did you react to those events when they coincided with your values?

Most people begin questioning the values they were given by their parents when they are away from home for the first time. Living away from home, whether in the military, in college, or in a new neighborhood for a job, offers the opportunity to examine values. It's usually during young adulthood that you are exposed to a variety of values. One of the tasks of adolescence is to differentiate yourself from your parents by figuring out which of their values you may not want to perpetuate. How did you do this? Did you do it early in life or later?

The first time you live with someone other than a member of your immediate family, your values come under scrutiny. Whether it's a roommate or a lover or a spouse, suddenly you are exposed to habits that are alien to you. In my family of origin, it was acceptable—even encouraged—to read incessantly. Reading while eating was permitted, reading while carrying on a conversation was permitted. When I ventured out into the world I was, rightfully, considered rude for attempting to read while someone was talking to me. I was astonished. "What? You don't value reading? And I thought you were an educated person. How could you not value reading above every other activity?"

Eventually, I realized that intelligence and good manners are not mutually exclusive, and valuing reading above all other activities is not necessarily a value to be proud of.

Sample

I grew up in a sports-addicted family. My parents and my sister were crazy about athletics and exercise and fitness. They ran to get the newspaper every morning from the front porch to see the team scores. They never missed a game in town and they used vacations to see games in other cities.

When I was a kid, I had no choice and I had to go along with them. I never enjoyed myself and wished I were back in my room with my Internet friends and my video games. I was considered weird.

Then I went away to college and found so many kids like me. By the time I went home for winter break, I had the confidence to tell my parents I wasn't joining them for sports events. They thought I was joshing. Then my sister said, "I always knew he was just going along. Just like I go along when it comes to religion." My parents stopped gaping at me and looked at my sister with horror, and our family was never the same after that day.

Sample

A cozy family life is what I came from. My parents lived near both sets of their parents and many aunts, uncles, and cousins lived within walking distance of us. They all assumed I would get a wife and move right into the neighborhood. I thought so, too. But then I started working and I loved my work and I wanted to work all the time. I got jittery just sitting around my family's living room on the weekends. I wanted to go to my office. That's when I moved to a downtown apartment away from the clan. Dating was not for me because I didn't want to invest time in a relationship when I could use that time for business. My family couldn't believe it, but it was true. I loved my job more than I loved the idea of making my own family. Anytime I wanted the warmth of relatives I could have it, but it wasn't that often. Mostly

I worked and I don't regret it one bit. All my nieces and nephews especially benefit because they are my heirs and I do make a lot of money that I don't have time to spend.

Sample

I went to Dr. Koren, a psychotherapist, when I was struggling to find myself as a young adult. One winter day she commented that I wasn't appropriately dressed for the cold weather. I explained that growing up in California I never had the heavy outerwear that is required here in New England but I was saving up to buy myself a coat.

"Why don't you go to the downtown coat store tomorrow?" she suggested. "They're having a 75 percent off sale on winter merchandise."

I replied, "In my family we don't buy things on sale. That's getting leftovers. If it's not good enough for rich people, it's not good enough for me."

Dr. Koren told me that she knew people, even rich people, who would never make a purchase if the item was not marked down. She said she knew people who lived for sales and bought things they didn't need just because they were on sale.

After I finished therapy I was a stronger person and I also dropped the idea that I could only buy things if they were full retail price. It seems stupid now but it was the way I thought I had to spend my money. Eventually, I realized I could make my own decisions not only about how I spend money but also about how I wanted to spend my time. You might say I was free to be my own person and form my own values.

Sample

I was so happy when Alan brought Rachel home for the first time. She was just what I pictured for him—pretty, smart, and interested in music just like he is. After we finished with all the small talk, Rachel chatted about shopping at Neiman Marcus, about staying at five-star hotels, and then she told us she drove a Jaguar. It's not that we couldn't afford those luxuries. My husband does very well in his business. But we would never waste money like that. I got annoyed at Rachel. Didn't she ever hear of Costco? How about Target? Didn't she know about regular cars? Apparently not. Alan could see I was upset and later he told me that Rachel's spending upset him, too, when he first met her. But now he tells himself that she earns plenty of money, she is not in debt, and she enjoys all her possessions and she enjoys shopping for them. So he has learned to respect her values and she has taught him to loosen up. I still wish she had my value of frugality.

Sample (from Murray)

Helping others was always a big deal in my family. My mother would make supper for kids in our apartment building who didn't have a good home life. My father would loan money to anyone who asked. I followed in their footsteps and didn't realize that the people who were asking for things from me were not good people. They were influencing me in terrible ways but I had trouble saying "no" to them. When Tommy gave me a big box and asked if I'd hold it in my room for him for a week I didn't think anything of it. I said, "Sure." It never occurred to me to look in the box. Only when the cops came to my door did I find out what was in there. I was helping others to the point of stupidity.

Sample (from Judy)

My parents both had a fine education in Europe and praised the intellectual life. When they came to America, they had trouble not only learning English but learning about day-to-day living. I wanted to follow in their footsteps and get a good education. Learning was very important to me and I signed up for classes that were way too difficult, and that turned out to be a good thing. I tried hard and I stayed up very late every night and I made honor roll by the time I was two years in America. I was proud but my parents didn't think it was anything special. They had no idea of the sacrifices I was making so that our family would be known as the family with brains.

You make choices and decisions every day without realizing that you may be expressing a long-held value.

Clear Communication: Latin Abbreviations

There are two Latin abbreviations authors often use. Those abbreviations are *i.e.* and *e.g.* Learn the difference between them and you'll never mix them up.

i.e. stands for *id est* in Latin, which translates to *that is*. Use it when you want to explain something to your reader with different words than the words you just used.

Each sentence below is expanded and clarified by the words after *i.e.*:

> *I just spoke to my best friend;* i.e., *Ellen.*
>
> *Rachel wastes her money;* i.e., *she buys way too expensive shoes.*
>
> *Len is very competitive;* i.e., *he loves to play sports all weekend.*
>
> *Abraham is a good music student;* i.e., *Abraham will practice for hours.*
>
> *My granddaughter, Katie (*i.e., *the one who lives in Cambridge), rides her bike to work.*

Note that the first part of your sentence usually ends with a semicolon, then comes the *i.e.* in italics, followed by a comma, and then the explanatory phrase or sentence.

e.g. is Latin for *exempli gratia,* which means *for example.* You can remember the meaning of *e.g.* by assuming the *e* stands for *example* and the *g* stands for *given—example given.*

See sentences below for examples of *e.g.* You'll notice that the examples are usually just one or a few of many in a list. The entire list—of friends, of fruits—is not mentioned.

> *I enjoy talking to my friends;* e.g., *Ellen, Barbara, Naomi.*
>
> *Rachel wastes her money;* e.g., *flying first class, throwing away leftovers.*
>
> *Karen eats fruit for breakfast;* e.g., *bananas.*
>
> *Peter enjoys almost all music;* e.g., *jazz, classical.*

After using *i.e.* or *e.g.* in a sentence you can check your accuracy by substituting *that is* for *i.e.* and *for example* for *e.g.* If it makes sense then you wrote it perfectly.

Day 10

To have hope is to create resilience. Hope gives strength. Dreaming about a good future helps you get through a difficult present. Fantasies that transport you to a place of calmness when the world around you is chaotic are healthy diversions. They protect you from succumbing to stressful circumstances. They give you hope.

What did you hope for? For some people, hope is similar to faith. Is that true for you? Your reader will want to know about the hopes you had as a child and the hopes you had as you matured. Are they the same? Do you still have those hopes today? Did you achieve them? Did you replace them? And what about your faith?

List the hopes you had in your life and in pursuit of your mission.

Sample (from Patricia)
Patricia is an artist who is following this memoir-writing program. You'll see examples of her writing throughout the book. She lists the hopes she had over the last years as:

> A home filled with glorious artwork
> A chance to study painting with Martin
> The opportunity to meet other artists
> Recognition for my work from art critics
> A show of my own in a New York City gallery

Sample (from Murray)

Murray, whom you've already met, is a teacher. His hopes as he entered adulthood were:

> Being a respected teacher
> Having a chance to help kids and prevent them from getting into trouble
> Living a clean life in a good neighborhood
> Having friends who never went to rehab and never went to jail

Sample (from Judy)

Judy, whom you've also met, is a young mother who came to the United States from Europe as a young girl. Her hopes were:

> To live the American dream
> To have a house in the suburbs with a backyard and a garden
> To have an American husband with a family that welcomed me
> To have children who would be smart enough to go to college and become professionals

Choose one or two of your hopes to write about at length. Let the reader know why you had these hopes and how you fulfilled them and how you felt once they were fulfilled. If your hopes were not fulfilled, let the reader know the efforts you made to succeed and how you handled your feelings of disappointment.

Sample (from Judy)

I wanted to live like I thought all Americans lived. It is not an exaggeration to say I expected gold in the streets. It was heartbreaking to arrive in the United States and live in a run-down apartment and see my parents who were professionals in Europe working as a maid and a chauffeur here. And my dad, the chauffeur, was actually illegal at driving because he never learned English well enough to pass the written portion of the test.

I tried everything to help my parents. Even though I was young I went to neighbors to ask if they wanted me to wash their dishes. I tried hard in school and I always got 100 percent on spelling tests because that was the only test where you got the answers in advance. I would memorize everything.

I loved learning and I wanted to go to college, so I knew I would have to do very well in school to get a scholarship. My parents wouldn't be able to help me with expenses. My disappointment in our situation just made me more determined to study and be smart and learn English and qualify for scholarships. My determination was strong. No one could stop me from studying.

Clear Communication: Confusing Words

Be careful when you use these words: *affect* and *effect*.

When you write about people who have impacted your life you are writing about people who have *affect*ed you. Think of *affect* as influence. If a situation influences you, it *affect*s you.

Then there is *effect*. The result of a situation is the *effect* of that situation. *Effect* can also mean the consequence of an action.

> *Your writing will* affect *your readers in a profound way because the daily writing that you do creates good* effects.
> *Cold weather always has a bad* effect *on me; it actually* affects *my ability to do my morning walk.*

And be careful when you use these words: *accept and except.*

When you *accept* the circumstances of your life, you are saying yes to those circumstances. When you do not tell your readers about certain incidents in your life you are excluding and *except*ing those incidents. *Except*ing means to leave out.

> *Please* accept *the idea that writers are* excepted *from paying for their own books at bookstores.*

Day 11

Thinking about what you've been through in order to wind up where you are today, list some of the milestones you reached along the way. Keep in mind the goal of your memoir—your mission. Recognize and write about your milestones to show your reader your accomplishments and how you achieved them.

Sample (from Patricia)
Patricia's purpose in writing her memoir is to show what she went through to achieve prominence in the art world. Her milestones were:

> Graduating from art school
> Getting married
> Giving birth to my twins
> Getting a divorce
> Having my first painting accepted at a gallery
> Speaking at the annual watercolorist event

Sample (from Murray)
Murray's purpose in writing his memoir is to figure out how he overcame his teenage problems and became a teacher. His milestones included:

Overcoming an addiction
Getting certified as a teacher
Giving up the old friends
Moving away from the old neighborhood

Sample (from Judy)

Judy's purpose in writing her memoir is to show how she adjusted to life in America. Here are her milestones:

Learning English
Becoming a citizen
Providing a true American life for my son

Choose one of your milestones and tell a story about it. Describe the circumstances and provide details and descriptions.

Sample (from Patricia)

I knew I'd have to leave Paul. If I stayed with him I'd never be able to develop myself as an artist and if I didn't have a way to express myself artistically I think there's a real chance I might have died. Certainly I would not have had a good life or a happy life and probably I would have thought about dying just to escape.

Paul hated art. I mean it. He couldn't understand why anyone would want to look at paintings if they could be looking at stock tables and charts. He didn't know why people went to museums if they could be visiting the stock exchange or their broker's office. Once the twins were in school he thought I should be getting a job. I wanted to paint and to study painting. There were fabulous art instructors in our city and I just knew I could qualify and get into a watercolor class. We didn't need the money. Paul made a good salary. He wanted me to plan lavish parties and vacations. That just wasn't for me. But I didn't want to cause the kids any trauma so I hung in there. I got a job, I planned parties, we went on elaborate vacations, we bought new cars, and I waited until the time was right. Then I announced that I was quitting my job to go to art school. Paul was disgusted with me. He tried to convince me to reconsider. And then the trouble began.

Sample (from Murray)

Giving up the old friends was not easy. It wasn't like I had any new friends. Those guys were my life. We knew each other since first grade at St. Michael's. We stood up for each other. We all knew each other's families and we ate with them all the time. But I was the only one of the guys to go to college and I was the only one to have a real job and I was the only one who was serious about staying away from booze and dope. I meant it and I wasn't going to drink or do drugs anymore. Most of the guys had money from doing odd jobs and from selling pills, but sometimes Joey was short and would hit me up for a loan. I hated to say no because he was like a brother to me. I knew that if I stayed in the 'hood I'd always be helping him. I knew about enabling and how wrong it was. But I was a coward. I couldn't say no. Finally, there was only one thing I could do to get rid of my old friends. I moved far away. It was not easy and they all hate me for it.

Sample (from Judy)

> Coming to America without one word of English was a challenge. But I figured out that television could be my teacher. On the weekends, from morning until night, and on school days from four P.M. to bedtime, I watched every sitcom and every newscast. I sat in front of the screen with paper and pencil so I could jot down words I would want to look up in the dictionary when I got to school the next day. I learned the intonations of English and the way words flowed. My television teachers helped me to more easily understand what my schoolteachers were saying. But my television teachers never used some of the words that the kids used in the school yard and the playground. I didn't hear those words anywhere else. But I did see them scrawled on walls in some public restrooms. Those were the words the kids would pay me a nickel to say to our principal. Lucky for me I never could find the principal.

Sometimes it seems that reaching a goal will take forever. Sometimes it seems that you will never accomplish what you set out to do. A useful technique is to divide your big goal into many small tasks. Think back to the days when you were reaching for milestones. Were you able to take actions a bit at a time with your eye on the goal? Show the readers how you did that, how you accomplished what you set out to do by taking baby steps when necessary.

For example, you might have felt overwhelmed if you were given instructions to simply write a memoir. But you are not overwhelmed when that goal is broken into thirty components. All you need to do is follow the instructions one day at a time. Each time you complete a day's assignment you have reached a milestone. Thirty milestones and you are finished writing what might have been too difficult to tackle all at once. Psychologists know that when a client seems overwhelmed, the trick is to make a plan of action divided into many small components. Now you know that trick, too.

Clear Communication: The Oxford (Serial) Comma

The Oxford comma. You may not know it by name, but you know it when you see it. The Oxford comma is the name given to the comma that puzzles us. Do we need it or do we skip it? It's the comma at the end of a list of items before the word *and*. It's before the last item and after the next-to-last item in a list. Is it necessary? Sometimes. The Oxford comma, also called the serial comma, is not used by every publisher. So, when you submit your manuscript to a publisher you can ask which style they prefer—with or without the serial comma.

> *I saw some interesting photos of a toothless grandmother, a jet-fighter pilot and a famous actress.*

Is the grandmother a pilot and an actress, too? The sentence above describes just one person.

Now see the sentence below:

> *I saw some interesting photos of a toothless grandmother, a jet-fighter pilot, and a famous actress.*

This sentence describes three people, each separated by a comma.

Use the Oxford comma to clarify your items in a list. If the meaning of your words is clear without the comma it is not mandatory that you use it.

> *Guests included Karen and Lewis, Judy and Peter, Lucy and David, Leah, and Joe.*

The commas in this sentence clarify that the first six people are actually three couples and the last two are not a couple.

> *We invited the pets, George Bush and Barack Obama.*

Here, the animals are named after presidents.

> *We invited the pets, George Bush, and Barack Obama.*

Here, the animals accompanied the two presidents.

Whenever you write sentences that include a list of items or names just read aloud and use a comma if and when clarification is needed. Using the words *and* or *or* to connect two items eliminates the need for a comma. The sentences below do not require commas:

> *We can leave on Saturday or Sunday or Monday.*
> *The little girl was hopping and skipping.*
> *I bought bagels and lox and bread and butter.*

The last sentence does not need a comma because *bagels and lox* and *bread and butter* are considered phrases and they are joined by the word *and*, which makes the meaning clear.

Day 12

You will hook your readers when you reveal the conflicts in your life and the ways in which you responded to those conflicts. The most compelling way to present your story is to write about a dilemma, a choice, a problem, or a trauma, and then about how you found resources within yourself to resolve the situation. Later on in your memoir, you can reflect upon your choices and proudly show off your new maturity and wisdom.

Your story shows your growth and transformation as you overcome hurdles and reach your goals. You may decide to write about circumstances that were unpredictable and then show how you responded to those surprising situations. Your reactions are the center of your story.

Is your life a soap opera? Is it amazing that you are still standing? Good for you; with the proper writing and marketing, your dramatic story may become a best seller. The late Frank McCourt (an unknown high school teacher until his memoir, *Angela's Ashes*, catapulted him to literary prominence) stated, in a six-word memoir, "A miserable childhood leads to royalties."

It is wise to remember that your flaws and failures are important. Don't write only about your successes, as tempting as that may be. Your readers need to know they are not alone when they mess up. They will take comfort in learning that you, too, had to struggle to overcome obstacles; you, too, faced disappointments. Writing about your struggles endears your readers to you; they continue reading because of the sustained crisis you portray.

Think about what you've been through in order to wind up where you are today. List some of the struggles you overcame along the way. Take the time to pull together all facets of your life to find an answer to the questions:

- How did I grow up to become the person that I am?
- What obstacles did I overcome?
- What struggles did I have?

After you identify your struggles, choose one or two of them to write about at length. Describe the full situation and explain the circumstances. You are the hero of your story.

- What actions did you heroically take to get what you want?
- How did you react to each obstacle?
- What are the risks you took in order to reach your goal?
- Your actions show your urgency and show you are at risk of not getting what you want.

When you think about your struggles, remember that the obstacles you have faced and overcome could have been either internal or external obstacles.

An internal obstacle begins in your mind. It emerges from your thoughts and ideas as attitudes or habits that can prevent you from reaching your goal. Some common internal obstacles include:

- Doubting you are worthy of reaching your goal

- Fearing failure so powerfully you prefer not to try at all

- Spending too much money

- Consistently rebelling against authority figures

An internal obstacle arises when reaching your goal requires you to do something that conflicts with your values. For example, you may have a long-held value of privacy yet in order to accomplish your goal, you may need to reveal personal information on Facebook, LinkedIn, and other social media. This conflict may prevent you from going ahead or may cause you extreme anxiety if you do proceed. How do you resolve this? That's the story your readers want to know.

Usually, it is our parents who give us our values, which are informed by our view of the world. You may notice you have the same internal obstacles your parents do. Many tendencies, habits, and simple likes and dislikes, come from your family of origin—whether by observing their behavior or through genetic predisposition. (When adults who were adopted at birth get to meet their biological family they often are astonished to see similarities not only in appearance but in life choices.) When writing your memoir, it's a good idea to recall the mannerisms of your parents, the activities they enjoyed, the foods they loved, the music that spoke to them, the ideas they embraced. You can jot down some of these memories and incorporate them in today's assignment or an assignment of another day. You may want to tell your reader about ways in which your obstacles are similar to and different from those of your parents.

An external obstacle begins in the outside world and has to do with circumstances over which you have no control, such as a job loss, a super storm, the death of a family member, a war, or an illness. Bad luck can happen to good people.

Your readers will be interested in and surprised by the obstacles you have overcome. Write about your internal obstacles and external obstacles.

Sample (from Patricia)

I struggled with learning how to charge a decent price for my professional services. I was taught to be self-effacing—you know, modest and humble and even meek. So how could I publicly declare myself an expert artist, especially a good one whose work is worth lots of money? Well, I couldn't. Honestly, I thought the earth would open and swallow me up if I charged more than just a few dollars for my work. It is still difficult for me to actually ask a customer to pay a hefty price for my work. I'm always afraid they'll laugh at me and tell everyone I had some nerve to charge so much. In my family, if we drew attention to ourselves in any way or said anything that could be misconstrued as bragging, we were immediately punished. Now I'm punishing myself because the competitive art world steps on artists who don't promote themselves. Self-promotion is very hard for me, not only professionally but in my personal life, too.

Sample (from Murray)

It was a big struggle for me to admit I had a problem and then to make amends to all the people I had hurt. It was a big struggle for me to work two jobs to make enough money for college tuition, and it was a bigger struggle and really tough for me to leave my neighborhood. The familiar people and places that I knew were not good for me were all that I knew and all that I loved. It took courage to pick up and leave.

Sample (from Judy)

As a foreigner, I knew it would be difficult to learn about popular culture. I never gave up reading magazines and trying to get with it. But when I was pregnant, I realized I didn't know enough about infant and baby rituals. Even before he was born, I knew that I wanted Georgie to be truly American. That's why we named him after the first president of the United States. One day while I was pregnant and waiting for my turn at the obstetrician's office, I noticed a pregnant mom there with a little girl about two years old. "They are singing songs," I thought at first. Then I realized they were reciting nursery rhymes. I recognized the rhythms but the words were not familiar to me at all. I did not know the rhymes and I was due to give birth very soon. Would my boy be the only kid in preschool who would not know his rhymes? No way. I panicked and on the way home from the doctor, I stopped at Barnes & Noble and bought a set of CDs that had one hundred nursery rhymes. From that day on, they were all I listened to. I listened in the car, I listened in the kitchen, I listened when I was walking. I even went to sleep with headphones. My husband is American and he says I know more rhymes than he does.

Judy describes the external obstacle of moving to another country. Luckily, she did not have the internal obstacle of believing it would be too difficult to learn rhymes in a language that was not her native tongue.

The public will read your story if it exemplifies a life lesson that resonates with them. Your family and friends will read whatever you write, particularly if they are in it.

And every reader, even those who do not know you, will enjoy your memoir because of your honest portrayal of your life. The personal emotional responses that you write about, in your unique writing style, provide the drama that will keep your readers interested in your story.

This assignment will fill your memoir with vivid action. Write dramatically to hold readers' interest, but remember that everything you write must be believable.

Clear Communication: More Commas

Commas help the reader understand what you mean and prevent misunderstandings. In the sentence below, without a comma, the reader wonders if school principals have become drug dealers:

> *Say no to drugs from the association of high school principals.*

With a comma, we know that the principals are okay:

> *Say no to drugs, from the association of high school principals.*

See these sentences and realize that commas are important:

> *1. Cindy, without her Don, is crazy.*
> *2. Cindy, without her, Don is crazy.*

In the first sentence, Cindy can't live without Don. In the second, Don can't live without Cindy.

1. *Hannah says Alyssa is the cutest girl in the class.*
2. *"Hannah," says Alyssa, "is the cutest girl in the class."*

In the first sentence, Alyssa is the cutest. In the second, Hannah is the cutest.

1. *We're going to eat Ben before the soccer game.*
2. *We're going to eat, Ben, before the soccer game.*

In the first sentence, Ben is lunch. In the second, Ben is invited to eat lunch.

1. *The school term ended sadly.*
2. *The school term ended, sadly.*

The first sentence indicates that something tragic may have occurred on the last day of school. The second sentence indicates that it is sad that there is no more school this year.

Day 13

Think about your family of origin. List the names of your parents, siblings, grandparents, aunts, uncles, cousins, step-relatives. Next to each name write a few words to describe them. Describe their positive as well as their negative attributes.

If your mission statement does not specifically involve your family, please apply this assignment to other people in other situations. You may answer in just one or two sentences, or if one individual inspires you to write a lengthy story, please go right ahead and do so.

Sample

Mother: tall, smart, generous, too talkative

Sister: beautiful, happy, selfish

Father: judgmental, hard worker, skinny, slick

Grandpa: sentimental, cries easily, cute, good singing voice

Aunt Gail: attractive, worries too much, conscientious

Uncle Dave: athletic, kindhearted, bald, fun-loving

Uncle Steve: studious, stingy, handsome

Cousin Annie: good sense of humor, good musician, blond, impatient

Sample

Here is a list written by a memoir student whose memoir is about his life at boarding school:

Roommate #1: Funny, casual, likable

Roommate #2: Difficult, fussy, cranky

French teacher: Elegant, private

Literature teacher: Too interested in my personal life, unconventional

Dorm parent Jim: Tall, scholarly, quiet

Dorm parent Kevin: Obese, good singing voice, talkative

Now think about yourself and indicate which of the descriptive words you have selected for others apply to you, too. The writing exercise below will help you recognize your traits, your habits, your true self. As you write your essays, please let your readers see those mannerisms and characteristics. They help define you. You might decide to reveal the answers to these questions within an essay about you and your family. This can be a long piece of writing, or you can write several distinct, shorter pieces.

- Who made you feel good about yourself?

- Who made you cry?

- Who made you laugh?

- Who embarrassed you?

- Who understood you?

- Who helped you decide which values and ideas and ideals are important to you?

- Who prevented you from easily achieving your dreams? How? What did they do or not do?

Sample (from Judy)

One of our neighbors gave me a subscription to *The New Yorker* for high school graduation and she treated me to a session with a psychic when I graduated from college. I still read *The New Yorker*. It means so much to me because that neighbor had faith in me that I would understand it and could appreciate it at a young age. Because of my interesting experience with her psychic, I never shied away from unusual people. That lovely neighbor exposed me to alternative points of view and I am a tolerant person today because of her influence.

Sample

It's crazy to think that I was so influenced by a relative I barely know but it is true. My parents and my sister and I were going to my cousin's birthday party by taxi. I had only been in a taxi a few times before and it seemed a little scary so I wrote down the driver's name and license number. My parents saw me copying that information from the ID card that hangs in the back of the taxi and they both got excited. "Stop it, what's the matter with you?" they shouted. "Why are you doing that? Can't you just relax? What's wrong with you?" they kept repeating.

I started to wonder if there was something wrong with me. How come I liked to be extra cautious? Was I defective in some way? I was worried all the way to the party. When we went in and sat down, there was a family there who I never met before. They had a son my age and the dad was telling a story. He was saying, "Jerry is so cute that whenever we get into a cab he copies down the driver's license information." And then that dad smiled at his son.

I know this sounds weird but I swear that hearing that conversation changed my life because it made me think I could be normal and maybe my parents were too critical and too quick to judge everything I did and find fault with me. From that day on, I had self-confidence when I did things that some people might think were a little peculiar. I honestly think that I am a successful scientist today because I didn't let my lab partners stop me from trying out new ideas even though they laughed at those ideas.

Sample (from Murray)

My mother was not a strong woman. She rarely ventured out of our apartment. In the apartment, she was totally in charge and felt good, but when she had to go out to any other place, such as my school, she became shy. She never thought she had the power to control me. One of my teachers, Mrs. Morgan, realized this and told me that she would guide me. She was my homeroom teacher and she thought I could be somebody. She told me to get away from the guys I was hanging out with and she told me to stop smoking cigarettes. I didn't listen to her. She said she didn't want to hear that I was in trouble and she didn't want to hear that I was doing anything to harm my health. Mrs. Morgan took the time to care about me and to let me know that she did. For years, when I was doing illegal things, I thought about her and sometimes felt ashamed and tried to stop because I knew she had better things in mind for me. She was always in my thoughts and, now that I'm writing this, I think I need to Google her and see if she's still with us. I hope so. Finally, she could be proud of me.

Words are powerful and even an offhand comment can influence another person.

Clear Communication: Fancy Words

Choose your words carefully and don't use five-dollar words. Five-dollar words are the ones you were tempted to put into compositions you wrote in elementary school in an effort to impress your teacher. Your readers are not interested in your fancy vocabulary words; they are interested in your story.

Use the precise word, not the pompous, pretentious one. In the sentences below the first versions are easier to read and convey the information just as clearly.

1. Here's what happened.
2. Here's what transpired.

1. My adventure began on a Tuesday.
2. My adventure commenced on a Tuesday.

1. I hope you agree with me.
2. I hope you concur with me.

1. I saw a stranger lurking.
2. I espied a stranger lurking.

Keep it simple.

Day 14

Thinking about your past and about the important decisions you have made in your life, please write about yourself using the phrases below, either in several separate essays or contained within one longer piece. Your readers are interested in your life. Tell them everything; don't hold back. As you write, think about how this information relates to your mission statement.

Please include these sentences in your writing:

I was shocked when I learned that not all mothers _____
_____*.*

I thought I was like everyone else, and then _____
_____*.*

What a surprise it was to find out that other fathers _____
_____*.*

I was so naïve, I thought it was perfectly normal that _____
_____*.*

My world turned upside down the day that _____
_____*.*

It was a relief to find out _____
_____*.*

Sample

I was shocked when I learned that not all mothers stayed in bed most of the day. When I was growing up, nobody mentioned the word *depression*. I just thought fathers went to work, kids went to school, and mothers stayed in bed. I thought it was normal that my father came home from work with shopping bags from the A&P and cooked for us. I thought it was normal that we often heard my mother weeping from behind the bedroom door. What kills me now is that my father and all our other relatives never thought of getting help for my mother. We loved her and accepted her exactly the way she was, which was a good thing but definitely not a helpful thing. It didn't help her get better. Nothing ever helped her get better. When I had a serious case of the flu, my mother got out of bed and took up residence in my room. She wanted to be close to me because she wanted to catch the flu, too. She prayed it would kill her.

The author of this memoir is a psychiatrist who traces his interest in psychiatry to his childhood. He writes about what it was like to grow up with a mentally ill mother.

Sample

What a surprise it was to find out that other fathers actually participated in family life. My father went to work at "the place" and then came home for dinner and watched sports on television and then fell asleep in his recliner. Most mornings when I got up for school, he was still on the recliner in front of the TV. I had a good childhood with my mom as my best friend and I was definitely her best friend because her husband was working or eating or sleeping so he was never available to her. The trouble began when I was ready to leave for college. Mom said I was abandoning her and then when my guidance counselor told her I should go away to college, she said it was okay to abandon her; she would find someone else to hang out with. And that's when she started up with Herb. My father accused me of causing their divorce, so I quit college and that was a big mistake. I was hoping they'd get back together. But everything went wrong and I wound up without an education and without a family home. That's when I decided to join the navy.

This writer's mission statement is: *I want readers to know what I went through in order to function and get ahead in the navy.* It is the story of his years as a United States sailor.

Sample

I was so naïve, I thought it was perfectly normal that every Sunday I helped my mother pack lunches and snacks and we drove for three hours to visit Dad. He was in a place called prison. I knew that word from the time I was little, and people asked where my father was or where I was going on a Sunday.

My mother explained, "Some people don't understand about prison. It's a place for good men who love their families so much that they borrow money from their boss to buy things for their family. Sometimes a mean boss doesn't want to loan the money so these guys have to do what they have to do to take care of their families. And that's why prison has some good guys living in it."

I believed Mom when she told me that a good family

man was the type who would do anything to get money for his family, even if it meant he couldn't live with them anymore.

This memoir is about the writer's childhood, specifically ages seven through eleven, when her father was incarcerated.

Sample

It was a relief to find out that my boss was well respected by other lawyers. Sometimes I got the feeling that he was a fraud, or at least a bit less than honest in some of his dealings. I wondered if I should quit my job. I didn't want to get into trouble. He allowed me to attend the annual national meeting with him this year and I got to see him in action. He wasn't sleazy and everyone applauded the cases he presented, even the judges. When he tells me to pay extra attention to certain clients and ignore others, he might have good reasons. I've tried asking him and he tells me not to worry. But the best attorneys in our state were all there congratulating him and telling him he is their idol. So, this might be my paranoia acting up again.

This writer's mission statement is: *My memoir is about what I went through in order to get off Medicaid and use my education at a real job and go to work every day even though I have a mental illness.*

How is your writing progressing? Are you finding it easier to make time to write each day? You're almost at the halfway point—good for you.

Clear Communication: Extra Words

Don't use two words when one word will suffice. Here are some examples of phrases that should be reduced to just one word:

> *Advance warning; warning*
> *As of yet; yet*
> *Close proximity; close*
> *Consensus of opinion; consensus*
> *Due to the fact of; because*
> *Every single; every*
> *Join together; join*
> *Meet together; meet*
> *Off of; off*
> *Totally flabbergasted; flabbergasted*
> *Until such time as; until*

When you write, believe in yourself and state your feelings without hesitation. If you feel tired say *tired*, not a *little tired*. If you feel *happy*, say *happy*, not *pretty happy*. Skip the word *very*. Are you organized? Good. Say it; don't say *very* organized. Is your friend furious? Say it; don't say *very* furious. And no entity can be *very* unique. *Unique* in itself is . . . well, *unique*.

Read the essays you've written and check your sentences to look for unnecessary words that can be eliminated.

Day 15

Please answer one or two of the three questions below. Use your memory, and especially use your heart.

1. Did you have a security blanket or other security object as a child? What was it? Were there issues related to your using it? When did you need it? What happened if you didn't have it?

Psychologists call these security articles transitional objects. These objects help a person make the transition from home and comfort and love, to a new and unfamiliar environment. You may have a transitional object with you. Do you have family photos on your desk at work? Do you carry family photos in your wallet or on your phone? Those photos are your transitional objects and help you, even when you are all grown up.

2. What were the best gifts you received, or gave, when you were a child? As you grew older?

Gift giving is part of every culture. Researchers have learned that giving a gift actually stimulates the pleasure center of our brains. We enjoy giving a gift to someone we care about and knowing we are pleasing them. Some well-meaning people attempt to use gift giving as a way to transmit values. This is admirable but could be misguided. The teenager who hoped for concert tickets might not appreciate opera tickets, just as the video-game aficionado might not appreciate a new book. Choosing the right gift takes time and thought. Many people today face a gift dilemma when wondering if everyone wants a gift card or if such cards are symbolic of lack of thought? Gift giving can be complicated.

3. Identify one or two love interests who were important to you in your teen years and other times, as well. Include idols or icons—real or imagined, dead or alive. Why did you love them?

Teenagers often become enamored of a celebrity. It is so much easier to have strong feelings for someone you will never really have to speak to than to express the feelings you might have for the classmate who sits next to you in algebra. Enthusiastically pursuing a popular figure helps the teen feel accepted as part of a group of fans. Liking the right idol is as important to some teens as is having the right hairstyle and the right jeans. It's part of establishing an identity outside of the family.

Your memories and feelings can generate an emotional response. Your answers to these questions create anecdotes that connect the reader to your deep emotional life.

Below are two examples in which each writer starts by responding to the question, and then veers off onto an unexpected path. The essay about gifts reveals an alternative lifestyle, and the essay about a popular singer turns into a discussion about the life of a juvenile delinquent. Both writers knew what they wanted to write about and the essay topics helped them begin the conversation in an original manner. You, too, can present information in an interesting fashion by starting your conversation with an anecdote that subtly leads to new information.

Sample: Best Gifts Received

Gifts were a source of embarrassment for me. At birthday parties, the other kids brought brightly wrapped store-bought presents with shiny bows and dangling ribbons. My parents, way ahead of their time, thought all that paper was an excessive waste of resources. So, the gifts I presented to my classmates at PS 28 were wrapped in newspapers. My mother said I should be proud of our recycling efforts. I thought I should drop the gift into an open sewer as I walked along the Grand Concourse on the way to the party.

But wait, there's more. No commercially produced offerings would emerge from our household. No sirree.

Since we had no television, we did have plenty of time. The family activity on an evening before a birthday party would be plaster of Paris moldings. Icky white paste . . .

The writer above had this mission statement: *I want the readers to know what it was like growing up with hippie parents who were antimaterialists and anticapitalists.*

Sample: Idols and Icons

I loved Eddie Fisher. I thought he had the cutest face, the best dimples, the sweetest personality, and the finest voice ever. I was president of the Eddie Fisher Fan Club, Bronx Division, back in the day. But then he ditched Debbie Reynolds for Elizabeth Taylor. And then he got divorced from Liz. And then he got married again and again and yet again. He stopped singing. He started drinking. And doing drugs. And still I loved him.

With Eddie, I wasn't just another fan, just another teenage girl. I was somebody. I was clever. I learned how to sneak onto the set of his nightly fifteen-minute TV show. I figured out how to bypass the doormen of his Essex House apartment building. My confidence exploded. I loved Eddie Fisher and I loved breaking the rules.

The writer above wrote a memoir about her years in a detention facility for adolescent girls.

Judy's excerpt below, on the other hand, demonstrates a straightforward response to the question.

Sample: Security Object (from Judy)

I thought I was totally assimilated into America. My son is a true American, as is my husband. I have no accent. I live in a typical American suburb. But I guess I've been deluding myself. After 9/11, when fear was in the air and foreigners were suspected of anything and everything, I felt like I might be in jeopardy. I wasn't even from a Middle East country, but I still felt that way. So, ever since then I carry my passport with me. Even to go to the gym, even to drive carpool, even to go for a walk, I take it. I need that security so that I can never be separated from my husband or my son or my beautiful America.

Whether you choose to change directions in your writing or not, as you reveal your memories, you entice the reader to want to know more about you and your life's journey.

Clear Communication: Their, There, and They're

Their, there, and *they're*: All three of these words have the same sound but each has its own distinct meaning.

Their shows possession and belonging.

> *Members of my writing class are writing* their *memoirs.*
> *They are busy reading* their *books about memoir writing.*

Read aloud and replace *their* with *our*. If that makes sense and could be a sentence then it is correct usage.

There refers to a place.

> There *is a staircase on your left.*
> *The students went* there *to hide.*

There is also used with the words *is* or *are*.

> There *is much to write about in a memoir.*

If you're unsure of usage read aloud and replace *there* with *here*. If the sentence still makes sense, you are correct.

They're is a contraction that stands for *they are*.

> They're *playing the piano in the music room.*
> They're *busy writing their memoirs in the office over* there.

Replace *they're* with *they are*. If the sentence still makes sense, you are correct.

Day 16

Identify a memory that you try not to think about. Why do you reject it—too painful? Humiliating? Frightening? Is it a long-held secret? Write as much as you can about that memory.

Write as if no one but you will ever read your words. Quickly put on paper those words that you're afraid to say aloud. If you weep while writing about this memory, you'll know you are onto something really good. Admit the truth and your story will be authentic and interesting. Always remember that truth is stranger than fiction.

When you show the reader one embarrassing incident that demonstrates how terrified or unstable you were at that time, the reader will identify with you, feel for you, root for you, and love you. Leave your pride out of this. Leave your dignity out of this. Your reader deserves raw reality.

Please don't write too much about the qualities most people wish for—a good, stable family; a successful career; a thin, trim body; a beautiful home; soaring self-esteem; many people who love and adore you. That will just bore your readers or make them envious. If those qualities are part of you, include them at the conclusion of your memoir. Most of your memoir should be about your problems. If you were an emotional wreck with more problems than your readers could ever dream of, they will enthusiastically recommend your book.

Sample

I think about the day that I broke my husband's heart and I feel so terrible. I don't know why I did what I did. I think it's because I was angry at him for the way he always treated our daughter. He favored our son and often said nasty comments to our daughter. But I never confronted him. He also wouldn't look at her. When she talked to him, he would continue watching TV. I would get burned up but I didn't want to start a fight with him. Now when I look back (this was many years ago) I know that we would have been better off having a fight or two. But I kept everything in until that day when I suddenly blurted out to him something that wasn't even true. He got so upset I thought he was having a heart attack. He turned red and then white and then he had to lie down and then he got sick to his stomach. He didn't want to ever touch me again or talk to me. We got divorced in a year. It was really stupid of me to tell a lie that was so serious. I guess I just wanted to hurt him when I said, "Before your brother died, we had an affair and he was a good lover."

Sample

I heard about girls who were gold diggers and I was afraid that my girlfriend was after my money. So, I didn't pay for anything for her when we went out. She paid for her own food and her own drinks and her own movie tickets. I feel like a jerk when I think about it. It's not like I was a kid in high school. I should have known better because I was a grown man. I can't think about it without hating myself because I acted like a stupid kid and of course I lost the girl. But it did make me try to figure out how I got that way. Why was I so sure girls were gold diggers? Why didn't I trust women?

Why did I ruin decades of my life by listening to crazy ideas? Who taught me to be suspicious of all members of the opposite sex? Well, keep reading and I'll tell you who.

Sample

I wish I didn't know about my son's heart condition. There's nothing I can do to help him and he lives 2,000 miles away from me. His wife takes good care of him and he's a doctor himself, but none of that helps me at night when I can't fall asleep because I'm worrying about him. I don't want to lose him. I don't want him to be sick. I don't want his children to grow up without him. If I didn't know about his condition, I'd be a much happier person. In my parents' day, the younger generation would protect the older generation from bad news. Not anymore. I protected my parents. I never told them when I was separated from my husband the first time. I never told them when my youngest flunked out of college. What was the point in upsetting them? The only good thing about me knowing about my son is that because we have no secrets, we feel close. When I kept things from my parents I had to keep my distance so that nothing would slip out. That's probably why we never were as intimate as other families. I would envy the grandparents and grandchildren who did lots of things with each other. We had to have distance so the grandparents wouldn't find out whatever it was we were keeping from them.

Sample (from Murray)

I have a secret and I will write about it here. When I was a young, wild man I went to a party where there were many beautiful girls who thought I was worth fighting over. And fight they did. I wound up going home with Nicole. I never saw her again but I heard she was looking for me when she found out she was pregnant. I have no idea if the baby was mine. But someone from the old neighborhood told me when she gave birth and I have the date and I am planning to go on to one of those websites where you can find a missing dad. I will register my name and the date of the baby's birth and if the kid finds me I will go for DNA testing. The kid would probably be in high school or even older by now. Just in case I wind up being a dad, I have to keep my life extra good, extra clean, extra everything.

Think about your days in school and you probably will come up with a humiliating incident. Think of divorces in your family and you will come up with painful incidents. Everyone has experienced difficult times. Let the world know how you dealt with one of these times and how it changed you.

Clear Communication: Apostrophes

This punctuation mark has two uses; it can indicate possession or it can indicate a contraction.

Possession: When someone possesses something, an apostrophe and an *s* is placed after their name: Harry's hat, Jennifer's jeans, Karen's kittens, student's memoir. If there is more than one student it would be students' memoirs—the *s* is added to the end of the word and then the apostrophe follows: the soldiers' uniforms, the referees' whistles.

Contractions: When two words are merged to form one word, the missing letter or letters are replaced by an apostrophe. *Let us* becomes *let's*; *does not* becomes *doesn't*; *is not* becomes *isn't*, *could have* becomes *could've*.

Check your writing to be certain you've placed your apostrophes in the right spots.

Plural words do *not* get apostrophes unless they are showing ownership. *Cats* is plural, no apostrophe. *Cats'* water bowl shows possession, the water bowl belongs to the cats, so the apostrophe is used.

Signs in stores and listings on menus often get this wrong. Here are some signs that I have seen:

> *Tourist's welcome*
> *No drink's allowed in store*
> *Thank's for your support*

These three are wrong. Very wrong. The apostrophe is not to be used when you are writing about something that is plural, with no possession.

Full disclosure: I broke up with a man I had been dating when he sent me a love letter. I broke up with him because of his apostrophes.

Day 17

Please write two essays, each beginning with one of the sentences below:

They liked me.

They never liked me.

Can you recall how you comforted yourself when you realized someone did not like you? Emotional regulation is the term that describes your ability to handle your response to an emotional situation. Your family teaches you which emotions are permitted and which are not. Some families think screaming, raging, weeping, and other loud reactions are acceptable, while other families prefer a stiff upper lip and silence when confronted with strong negative circumstances. What did your family teach you? Did you continue in that mode? Let your readers know about you and your emotions.

Today's assignment gives you an opportunity to show your reader an aspect of yourself you've not yet discussed because each first sentence can lead to many possible scenarios. No matter the theme of your memoir, you can use *they like me* and *they never liked me* to introduce your readers to people and situations you've not yet described. You can reveal a valid reason why someone would not like you or you can describe how wonderful it felt to walk into a place of business, a retail store, a certain person's home, a classroom, a boardroom, a gym, a bar, or a restaurant, and know you were welcomed and well liked. Perhaps you can remember days back in grade school when a habit of yours turned your classmates against you, or you might recall the joy of feeling popular in high school, and the emotional compromises you made to remain at the center of the crowd.

Sample

They liked me. I was nervous about taking my first trip by myself since the divorce. I'd be in a strange country with people who were strangers to me but I summoned up my courage and I did it. When I walked into the hotel and my entire tour group was already assembled in the lobby, I realized I had gotten the time wrong and I was late. But it didn't matter. They welcomed me. Everyone smiled and extended themselves to make me comfortable. I was the only solo traveler in the group. But I had a great vacation and it was clear that they liked me.

This is the beginning of a travel memoir where the author confronts her fears about being single.

Sample

They liked me. Finally I met people who liked me and respected me and wanted to hang out with me when I was accepted to the music academy. All the other students were serious about music and no one thought it was weird to spend about eight hours every day practicing. If I knew a place like the academy existed when I was younger, at least

I would have had something to look forward to. Serious music students are in a class by themselves. We are all crazy about listening to music and making music and we don't go for a lot of the popular music that's around now. I thought I'd have it made and the rest of my life would be good from now on. But it didn't turn out so good. I had to leave the academy and it was very hard to do that. Suddenly, I was forced to be in escape mode, and it was all because of a mistake my father had made many years ago.

This writer's mission statement: *I want to tell the world how I became a well-known percussionist even though my father had ruined the career of a world-famous musician and I had the same name as my father.*

Sample

They never liked me. Some people are never satisfied. Just my luck those people were my family. I always had a feeling they didn't like me but then I found out my feeling was true when I was in the lawyer's office and she was reading the will. My sisters got everything, and my parents gave me five dollars and that was it. I used to wonder if I was adopted and they were sorry they got me. I snooped around when I got older to look in all their files and papers in the back closet and one day I hit pay dirt. It explained why they never liked me. After that, I didn't blame them so much.

In this tell-all memoir that reads like a mystery story, the writer exposes family secrets.

Sample

They liked me and I was so surprised. When I joined the air force I was sure I'd be a victim of taunting. I had heard a lot of rumors about mistreatment of women. Instead, I was respected and the officers treated me like anyone else. My being a woman did not get in the way of my achieving what I set out to accomplish. My experience was so good that I stayed and made the air force my full career. When I was sent to Okinawa, things got interesting. That's when good luck and good timing joined together and I was accepted to be part of a very special program. You'll be amazed when I explain that program to you. I can't tell you everything because some parts are secret. But in general, I was part of a team that did high-level work that made a big difference to our country.

This writer's memoir focuses on her special duties in the air force and the many countries in which she did her work.

Sample (from Judy)

They never liked me. Today I think it's just fine that I am serious and studious and smart. My husband thinks so, too. But when I was a kid, there was no support for someone like me. When no one wanted to pick me for a team or sit with me in the lunchroom, I felt sad and rejected and not one teacher ever said an encouraging word. If someone told me, when I was sitting alone, that it was okay to take out a book and read I would have been happy. I didn't need the other kids but I didn't like being ostracized. Nowadays, whenever I am awarded a prize for an academic achievement, I always mention in my speech that I was so alone in Glendale School and I ask all the audience members to be on the lookout for such kids today and help them recognize their good qualities.

Judy's memoir is about her struggles as an immigrant.

Choose memories from your childhood, your adolescence, or your adulthood. You might recall a crowd of kids or you might write about neighbors or a job or members of your family. If you cannot remember exact dialogue that's okay. Write about what probably would have been said to you.

Clear Communication: Capitalization

Use a capital letter to begin the name of a particular person, not any person. You would write *my uncle* (no cap), but you would write *Uncle Bill* (caps because you are referring to a particular person). The same rule holds for titles, streets, and institutions. These sentences are all correct:

> *The bank on Elm Street is closed today. Wells Fargo Bank, which is down the street, is closed today.*
> *Fifth Avenue is the most fancy avenue in the city. New York City has many fancy avenues.*
> *Westfield High School is closed for spring break. The high school in our town is closed this week.*
> *She missed her mother and her father. Mother Jane and Father Joe are away on vacation.*
> *Senator Josh Jacobs is speaking at tonight's meeting. Josh Jacobs, the senator from New Jersey, is speaking tonight.*

Day 18

Occurrences and confrontations during your adult years should be included in your memoir if they have made a change in the way you think or behave.

One incident can make a big difference in your life. Write about something that happened in your life that changed your way of thinking. When you write about your incident, please let the reader know where the scene is taking place and who else is there. Describe everyone and then describe everything you can see from where you are. Let the reader know about the weather, the time of day, even the year it is. Most of all, let the reader know what you are feeling. What conflict is important in this circumstance?

Each of the memoirists below has provided an excerpt from their account of a pivotal moment.

Sample

I wanted to have a great car, a big bank account, and a lavish lifestyle. Here's what was in my way: I had no skills and no job and no higher education and no idea how to earn a living. More obstacles than any one person should have. It probably meant that my expectations were totally unrealistic. But I knew I was a hard worker and people liked me.

I thought for a long time and I figured out how to get to live in The Towers—the fanciest building in our city, how to drive a late-model luxury car, and how to start accumulating money in my bank account. And I did not do anything illegal.

I read up on how to be a butler and I went to an employment agency for household help. They didn't have a butler job for me but they did have a job as a manny. A manny is a male nanny. I got the job and to this day I am still in touch with that family. I can't say their name because they are very rich and very famous. I lived with them for seven years, from the time their son was five until he went away to boarding school. I had my own bedroom and bath in The Towers; I drove their Mercedes whenever I needed to take the boy someplace; I skied with the family every winter, went to the Hamptons with them in the summer, and accompanied them on all their European vacations. All the while I was stashing away my salary because room and board came with the job. I accomplished my goal and I have some very interesting stories to tell. Resourcefulness is my motto.

This memoir describes the author's life as a manny. The moment he realized that this was a way for him to have all the things he wanted he focused on that goal and totally changed his life.

Sample

In my thirties, I wanted to take care of my father. He took such good care of me and my mom and my brother and sister when we were growing up. Now he was alone and sick. But how could I do that? I had two small children, a job, a husband, and a house to take care of, all about 200 miles away from Pop. My husband felt bad for me because I was sad after every phone call with Pop, and I never before used to cry or walk around wringing my hands. Don knew we had to do something but neither of us could think of what to do. Then at church one Sunday, the pastor started talking to me and I told him the cause of my great unhappiness. Within two days he had a solution. All because I let him know I was hurting. It was many years before I realized his solution hurt me even more.

This writer's mission statement: *My memoir describes what I went through to get away from a pastor who was taking advantage of me.*

Sample (from Judy)

My son often has school friends over at our house and one day I noticed a boy looking kind of guilty. As a mom you become aware of different faces that mean different things. This boy was up to no good but I couldn't figure out what exactly he had done. I couldn't just ask him to leave my house. My son said I was being paranoid and my husband thought I was overreacting. But I stood my ground and wouldn't let him out of my sight. He suddenly jumped up and said he had to quickly leave for home, and asked me to drive him. I happily did so and when I returned my son and husband showed me what fell out of the boy's pocket when he ran toward my car: lots of candy and gum that he had swiped from the corner store. I was happy because it confirmed for me that I know kids and I know when to be concerned about them. Since that day, I listen to my inner voice and not the voice of my husband, son, or friends. I've learned to believe in myself when I think something or someone is not right.

Clear Communication: Sentence Beginnings

When you were in school, your teacher insisted you must never begin a sentence with the words *and* or *but*. That was good information when you were learning to express yourself. It is not good information for you today. Mrs. Milrod is not looking. You may begin sentences with those words. In fact, *but* is a useful word with which to begin a sentence because it permits the reader to hear the other side of the story. Instead of using many words to explain an idea that no longer works you can simply say *but* and get right to your argument.

> *I am a quick writer. But I do understand that you may prefer a slower pace. Writing is a joy for me. And another point I want to make is that writing is often therapeutic.*

Beginning a sentence with the word *and* creates a rhythm to your words. If you decide to use it to begin a sentence be sure it is a true sentence and not a fragment. Also, be sure to read the entire paragraph aloud. Keep the word in only if it helps the flow and rhythm of your writing.

> 1. *I am a fusspot when it comes to grammar. And spelling, too.*
> 2. *I am a fusspot when it comes to grammar. And I also am particular about spelling.*

In the first example above, the sentence beginning with *and* is incorrect; it is a fragment and could not stand alone as a sentence.

In the second example above, the sentence beginning with *and* is correct; it makes sense and could stand alone as a sentence.

Day 19

Are you a memoirist who is curious to figure out why your mission was so important to you? Do you wonder why you chose certain actions to accomplish your mission?

If so, then today is your day to think back to an earlier time and recall:

- What made you angry?

- What was your secret desire?

- Who loved you?

- Did you crave attention? Were you shy?

- What frightened you?

- When did you feel most content and secure?

- Who influenced you in a positive way?

- Who influenced you in a negative way?

Please write whatever comes to mind as you ponder the above questions. When you write about your younger self, include incidents that you now realize were pivotal and helped you figure out something about life. Write about events that taught you a new way of looking at the world or a new way of looking at yourself.

Sample

> In high school, I loved Barry. He was cute and he was smart and he asked me out for New Year's Eve. I said yes, yes, yes. But my dad said no, no, no. Dad would not let me date a boy with a car. It didn't help that when Barry came over to my house for the first time I had warned him that my dad had a thing about me going out with a boy who was a new driver, so he wanted to reassure my father and he said, "Don't worry about your daughter driving with me. I'm a good driver and I'm not a new driver. I've been driving for four months." That didn't go over big. But I was determined to spend that fabulous evening with the boy of my dreams and I figured out how to do it. By the time I was a junior I was an excellent manipulator. My troubles with listening to authority figures began when I was in high school and truth be told, I still have those troubles.

This writer's memoir is about her career on Wall Street and the legal difficulties she has had.

Sample

> My family is still in my homeland but I am here in America. The only way I am strong enough to be without them is that when I was younger they gave me a lot of support and encouragement. My mother always said I would wind up in America one day and she said it with a smile on her face. I thought I might stay in the Azores but there is so much

more opportunity here. She is proud of me and I email her photos of my passengers so she can see that I am working with responsibility. Driving a taxi in Philadelphia gives me a chance to see the Liberty Bell every day and I am trying to pass my tests to become an American citizen. Starting when I was a small boy I wanted to make my mother proud and I still do.

This writer's memoir is about his quest to become an American citizen, despite the obstacles he faces every day.

Sample

I liked Miss Piggy from Sesame Street and I'm sure she liked me. I used to think she was looking right at me from the TV. I would get mad when my older sisters said that Miss Piggy couldn't see me. When they teased me about Miss Piggy, I would cry until my mom or my dad would rescue me from the rec room and take me to the kitchen for a snack. Snacks cheered me up. As a matter of fact, they still do. Sitting at the kitchen table with goodies spread before me made me feel content and secure.

The Miss Piggy memoirist is writing about his relationship with food, about his obesity, about his bariatric surgery, and his ultimate regaining of one hundred pounds.

Sample

My parents would never ever give me permission to smoke. They never smoked. But I figured I could smoke and they'd never know. By the time they each got home from work,

I'd freshen up the air in the house and get rid of my smell by eating and I just knew I could get away with it. But it was not to be. Whenever one of the cool kids handed me a cigarette, I would take a drag and immediately start coughing then choking then getting dizzy. It never failed. I was not meant to be a smoker but all through high school I tried and never gave up even though my efforts were in vain. I was desperate to be part of that crowd of kids, so I thought of another thing to do that I might succeed at and then I could be one of them. That was even more risky but it worked.

This writer tells readers about his teenage girlfriend's pregnancy and his experiences as a teen father.

Sample (from Murray)

I always felt most secure when I had alcohol with me. I didn't have to be drunk but I did need to know that there was a bottle nearby, even a can of beer would do. This started when I was very young, maybe eleven or twelve years old. If I knew I could take a sip of alcohol when I needed it, I would be brave and I could talk to anyone. If I had to confront a social situation without any alcohol I felt scared and I felt shaky. My security for many, many years came from drinking.

As you write today's assignment, show your readers what influenced you—something may have disturbed you, or something may have fascinated you—when you were younger. What events had an effect that is evident today? What circumstances persuaded you to make certain life decisions? What inspired you to make certain choices? Let your readers know what was important in your past.

One memoirist wrote about how distressed she was when relatives with babies and toddlers came to visit. She showed that she was upset by the mess in the house and then used that as a transition to lead into her memoir of life with obsessive-compulsive disorder. Another memoirist began with a description of how strange it was to stay in a hotel that had warped floors and very low ceilings, and then he went on to write about his life as an architect. A fashionista will have strong feelings about clothing and shoes and perhaps hair and makeup, too; a librarian will be concerned with books and magazines and information. Your personality is revealed to the reader by the incidents you choose to report. And remember that for now you are simply writing essays. Tomorrow, you'll be instructed on how to put them together in particular sequences to create your full memoir.

Clear Communication: Clichés

Certain expressions are overused and overworked and just plain boring to hear or to read. With a little effort you will come up with original phrases to describe the same circumstances that these clichés describe. Please do not put these phrases in your writing; in fact, avoid them like the plague. (Did you get it? *Avoid them like the plague* is a cliché.)

> *Afraid of my own shadow*
> *As old as the hills*
> *Busy as a bee*
> *By the seat of his pants*

Dead as a doornail
Few and far between
Fit as a fiddle
Green with envy
Hard and fast rule
It goes without saying
Like a kid in the candy store
Nutty as a fruitcake
Out like a light
The pot calling the kettle black
The tip of the iceberg

Please eliminate all clichés from your writing. You can have fun thinking of substitute sentences. Using clichés is a lazy person's habit because it requires no creative thinking. Fortunately, you are a creative thinker and you can come up with interesting, original phrases.

Day 20

Your memoir needs a plot. A plot consists of events that are linked to one another. One event leads to another in a logical sequence. The cause and effect are apparent. In your memoir, the events, which constitute part of the plot, cause some emotion in you and show the feelings you experience as you attempt to achieve your goal. The events of your plot show the actions you take to overcome the obstacles, both internal and external, that keep popping up to prevent you from fulfilling your mission.

A plot differs from a story.

A story is: You bought a book on how to write your memoir, you wrote some essays, you wrote about your childhood pet dog in some of your essays.

A plot is: You bought a book on how to write your memoir, you wrote some essays, now you understand why you cry whenever you watch a movie with a dog in it. You recall how much you loved your dog and you recall the cruel neighbor who despised Rex. You recount what you went through to keep the neighbor away from the dog and to achieve your goal of becoming a dog trainer.

The plot connects events via emotions, reactions, and responses. When you read the essays you've written, you'll realize your plot has suspense and conflicts, but usually only one goal. All your action is geared toward your quest, your mission.

The more obstacles and conflicts you include in your memoir, the more your reader gets hooked in. You want your reader to be in suspense and to continue reading. You want your reader to wonder if you will reach your goal and if so, how you will do it.

Today is the day you will gather all you have written and organize your writing to create what is called a narrative arc. The narrative arc is the story line that has a beginning, a middle, and an ending. In many ways, it is the plot; the plot is the summation of the cause and effect actions that are within the narrative arc.

Please print out everything you have written since Day 1 and then add any blog or personal journal entries you may have written that are relevant to this memoir. Have it all in front of you.

The beginning of your memoir is about your mission statement. It will let the reader know why you are writing this memoir. The beginning includes everything you want to show your readers about you to help them understand how you got to be the person who went on this particular quest.

The middle of your memoir is about the obstacles you faced trying to achieve your mission. Your internal and external obstacles are in this section. The people who hindered you and those who helped you are in this section, too. This section is full of activity and events. You will include all the actions you took to try to overcome the complications you encountered. The middle section of your memoir is the longest section.

The ending is an assessment of who you are today and how your experiences made you the person you are. In the ending, you will reveal the ways in which you have changed. You will show how your mission statement is fulfilled. Often, the ending of a memoir is the briefest of the sections.

Please read all your writings and label each page with a B for beginning, an M for middle, or an E for ending. Some memoirists—yes, you are now a memoirist—use sticky notes, others simply write on each page.

After you've divided the pages into three distinct groups of writings—those that will comprise the beginning of your memoir, those that will be the middle, and then those in the final section—please read your writings. Do you want to combine certain essays to create one long one? Do you want to redo certain writings to more clearly state your ideas? This is the time to do that.

If on certain pages there is not enough tension and not enough conflict, create more by thinking of incidents from your past and adding them in. Your reader is eager to read about your actions and the interesting events of your life. This is your time to enhance each essay you have written and come up with some new ideas, too.

As you read through your writings, please have the following questions in mind:

- Is it clear that you are eager to reach one particular goal?

- Is it clear that there are hindrances blocking your way?

If either of these is in doubt, today is the day to remedy that and add more information.

Congratulations! You have put together the first draft of your memoir.

To see how these separate pieces of writing can come together into a whole, take a look at the sample below. Robert has written his assignments each day and on some days combined a new essay with one from a previous day. I'll say no more and let Robert's writing introduce him to you.

Sample

> I started out in poverty, but had loving parents. I worked hard to become wealthy. Then I had to work even harder to have good relationships within my family.

Robert's initial three-sentence memoir.

> My memoir describes what I went through to be successful both in business and at home.

Robert's mission statement.

> What I most remember about my early life is being hungry. There was never enough food and me and my brothers had huge appetites. One day my mother put a potato on the table and it was the last food we had in the house. My father would be getting paid the next day and then we'd have more food. So my mother cut the potato into four slices. One for my father and one for me and each of my brothers. Now that I think about it, she did not have a piece for herself. Anyway, I was so hungry that I gobbled my piece in two seconds and then I saw my brothers' pieces and I started to cry. Immediately, my father handed me his piece of potato and said, "This is yours. It dropped and I just picked it up." I'm sorry to admit that I took it.

This is one of Robert's early memories.

> I had a teacher who threatened me every time I came to school without a handkerchief. In those days, we had inspection every morning. We had to show that we had clean

fingernails and a hanky in our pocket. I think they did this because so many of the families, like mine, were from other countries. It was a way to teach the immigrant parents about American hygiene and health habits. My family was perfectly clean but we didn't always have a handkerchief for me and for my brothers. So one day I would bring it in and the next Stephen would and the next Michael would. On the days I didn't have it my teacher would say that I was sure to get polio. Of all things to say to a little boy that was the worst. This was before the polio vaccine and there were epidemics all the time. We heard scary stories about kids in iron lungs and other kids who died. I wasn't sure if I should believe her but I didn't want to take any chances so I came to school with a piece of garlic tied on to a string and wore it like a necklace around my neck. I wasn't the only one. Many mothers believed that you could prevent your child from getting polio by hanging garlic around the neck.

This is the memory of a humiliating and frightening teacher.

Note that Robert informs the reader about the social and cultural milieu in which he grew up by recounting incidents. He does not blatantly state the year or his socioeconomic status, but allows the reader to infer that information.

When I was sixteen years old the kids I went to school with went to the movies every Saturday. They flirted with girls and sat in the balcony and sometimes in a section called the loge, and they smoked cigarettes. I wanted to go with them but I didn't have money for the movies, I didn't know how to talk to a girl, and I was scared of cigarettes. I also knew cigarettes cost too much for me. So I walked up and down Belmont Avenue and went into every store asking if they needed help on Saturdays. By my third Saturday of walking in and out of stores someone said yes.

A milestone for Robert.

Belmont Luggage sold valises. That's what we called suitcases then. Valises were a brownish color and made of a hard material. I don't think it was plastic because I don't think plastic was invented yet. They were heavy to lift but most people hadn't yet been on an airplane so they just used their luggage in their cars or on buses or trains.

It was my job to sweep the floor and sweep the sidewalk in front of the store, too. Then when a customer wanted to see a particular valise, I got it down for him. Nowadays, I could never hire someone as young as I was then and I would never allow any employee to climb up on shelves to bring down merchandise. But that's just what I did. I loved my job and my parents were so proud of the money I brought home to them every Saturday. I felt like the breadwinner along with my father and it was a fabulous feeling. I felt like a man, and I felt like an important man who had a purpose. Soon, I started working in the store after school, too. It was true good luck that my first job was such a good fit for me and that my boss took an interest in me. That job turned out to change my life. I loved that store. I wanted to be Mr. Belmont Luggage. The smell of the leather, the shiny floor, and the door that creaked whenever a customer walked in, all seemed like home to me. As the years went on and I graduated from high school,

I got to work there full-time except for when the owner's son returned home from college. I would be laid off for the whole summer and a couple of weeks during the year, too. It got me so upset I threatened to quit more than once. But the boss knew I wasn't serious. He knew that working for him was the best part of my life. During those summers when I couldn't work at Belmont, I got jobs in other luggage stores. None of them were as good as Belmont but I did learn from working in other places. For instance, I learned that people shoplift and I learned that you can't keep your eyes on the register and all your inventory and also talk to customers and that was why I was necessary in the store. My boss couldn't do it all by himself. My best day was when his son admitted he didn't want to work in the store. He wanted to become a druggist. A pharmacist as you would say today.

Memories of good luck and gratitude.

I heard my parents and other relatives talk about people they admired and those people were business owners who had fancy houses and fancy cars and seemed so independent. Even though they worked hard, they didn't have to answer to a boss. They were their own boss. I worked hard, never took a vacation, never gambled or drank, just saved money and, after some years, I was able to become a partner in the business. Eventually, I bought out my boss and Belmont Luggage was all mine.

Robert's family's values of hard work and independence are shown here.

I worked and worked and worked and created a great business. Of course I did it for my family as well as for me. I met Rose when we were young; I knew we would get married one day. I loved her from the beginning. We were a team just like my parents were. And sure enough, we married and had two kids. My children grew up in the store. We lived right there, above the store, when they were young, before I made enough for us to buy that first house. I always told my boys how lucky they were. I told them I didn't have a family member to help me and take me into a business. I had to work hard and then I saved for a long, long time to buy my way in.

Robert waits for the right time to pursue his goal.

You can imagine how I felt when my sons both told me they didn't want to work with me. They didn't like retail, they said. Just like that. It felt like someone sucker punched me. And how did they want to earn a living? They didn't know. "But don't worry, Dad. We'll figure it out," they said.

Robert has a confrontation with his sons.

Don't worry? They tore my heart out. What was I gonna do, hire someone else's kids to run the business? I hate to admit it, but for a couple of years I couldn't even look at my sons or talk to them. I wouldn't go to the phone when they called. I didn't want to see them because they made me sick. Then they actually told me they never liked me. "Oh, Dad, we love you. But you know we don't really have much to say to you. You're on a different page. You've always been on a different page."

What? A different page? What got into these kids?

Robert was shocked by his sons' ideas.

And then my wife, for the first time in our marriage, didn't stick with me. She said, "Robert, the train is leaving and I'm getting on it. I want to be part of our boys' lives. I don't want to miss their weddings, their babies, their everything. So, I'm going to be with them, visit them, talk to them, and if you don't want to get on board that's your problem."

This was a frightening experience for Robert.

This scared me. Rose, my partner, not being by my side and not supporting my decision made me feel frightened in a way I never felt before. If we weren't a team, what was the sense of going on? I said that to her and she thought I was going to kill myself. I wasn't but it did cross my mind during that week. What would be the point of having a good day in the store if I couldn't come home and talk to Rose about it? She was my right arm and I needed her. I guess you could say we needed to be on the same page.

At that moment, Robert realized he had to make some changes in his life.

Well, it took me a long time to realize she was right about our sons. After a couple of years, and a few good sessions with a shrink, I finally did realize it. And then we went to a family therapist and it changed everything.

Making that shrink appointment was the hardest thing I ever did. I felt like a courageous hero when I finally made the call after carrying around the phone number in my wallet for weeks. Talking to a stranger about family business went against everything I believed in. It was not weeks, to tell the truth, it was months since Rose had given me the name and number.

Those sessions were spiritual experiences.

What a surprise it was to find out that plenty of other fathers had kids who did not want to go into the family business. After those sessions, I understood that my boys had choices I never had because they had a totally different upbringing than I did. If only I could have figured all this out years earlier, we would all have been better off. In retrospect, I know that Rose figured it out. She knew way before I did that kids can break the pattern of following their father into the family business.

Robert examines his patterns and expectations.

I was under the illusion that hired help in the store would steal from me and I didn't want to hire anyone. But finally, I hired a good manager and then another good one and I let my kids do what they wanted to do. It worked out. They accepted me back into their lives.

They each have kids and guess what? Those kids love the luggage business. They work for me during their summer breaks from college and they are training with my managers. Eventually, the business is theirs. The best part is my two grandchildren are girls, or as they would say, women. I'm very proud of them. And I must admit I'm proud of myself. I risked everything I ever believed in by going to the shrinks.

Robert reveals his hopes.

Robert plans to write about several sessions within the therapist's office and also about how he arranges for his managers and his granddaughters to work together. He wants to show how he uses the relationship skills that he learned in therapy when he deals with his business staff.

Clear Communication: Quotation Marks

Quotation marks indicate conversations. Put quotes around the actual words that the person speaks and start a new paragraph for each new speaker. Do not use quotation marks if you are not quoting the exact words. A sentence that needs quotation marks is: *Joe said, "I am hungry."*

A sentence that does not need quotation marks is: *Joe said he is hungry.*

Except in rare circumstances, all punctuation marks are placed within the quotation marks.

> *"I look forward to reading your memoir," said Jack.*
> *"It's not yet finished," I replied, "but you will be notified when it is all done. I hope I finish it in two weeks."*

"How can you write it so quickly?" asked Jack.
"I just follow my daily program and it works."

Remember: new speaker, new paragraph.

In addition to showing what someone is saying, quotation marks are also used to identify the title of short pieces of writing—e.g., articles, short stories, short plays. Books, movies, and plays do not get quotes but instead get italicized or underlined. *I read a review of the play* Fiddler on the Roof, *and the critic particularly praised the song* "If I Were a Rich Man," is a sentence with correct usage.

Another use of quotation marks is to call attention to the inappropriate or ironic use of a word. When you are speaking, you would do this with your fingers, making air quotes. The quotation marks in this situation tell the reader that you realize the word is being used in a peculiar way. Here are two examples:

The cafeteria "food" was inedible.
Professor Lyons shared his "wisdom" with us today.

When you use quotation marks for this purpose they are called scare quotes, and they reflect your skepticism of the word you are describing.

Day 21

Today you will work on your beginning section.

The most important sentence in your entire memoir is your first sentence.

Please locate one sentence in all your B pages that will hook readers and entice them to keep reading. Don't start with an explanation or introduction. Instead, start with a dramatic incident that exemplifies your journey toward your goal.

Here are some first sentences of well-known memoirs:

1. *I was sitting in a taxi, wondering if I had overdressed for the evening, when I looked out the window and saw Mom rooting through a Dumpster.*

2. *At the age of 80, my mother had her last bad fall, and after that her mind wandered free through time.*

3. *My sharpest memory is of a single instant surrounded by dark.*

4. *Maybe it all began with a bug bite, from a bedbug that didn't exist.*

5. *I wish Giovanni would kiss me.*

Here are their sources:

1. *The Glass Castle: A Memoir*; Jeanette Walls, Scribner, 2006
2. *Growing Up*; Russell Baker, Signet, 1992
3. *The Liars' Club: A Memoir*; Mary Karr, Penguin, 2005
4. *Brain on Fire: My Month of Madness*; Susannah Cahalan, Free Press, 2012
5. *Eat, Pray, Love*; Elizabeth Gilbert, Penguin Books, 2007

Note how each author piques your interest without disclosing background information. You want to keep reading to find out who the author is and where the action is taking place. You already have the feeling that something significant is transpiring.

Look through your writings to locate a gripping sentence. Many memoirists have a first paragraph that is a dramatic incident that took place late in their journey. In subsequent pages, they then write about an earlier time and from there they proceed to fill in necessary information.

Your first few paragraphs might leave your readers wondering what's going on, and that's acceptable. The background information, called the backstory, is not necessarily at the very beginning of your memoir. It's more important that you hook the reader with some drama. Later on, you can reveal memories and recollections.

The beginning of your memoir will show the reader your thoughts, your feelings, and your actions during one particular time of your life. If you need to, add some more stories and anecdotes and memories to help the reader figure out why your goal is so important to you. Your actions will help the reader know that you have a serious desire for your goal without you explicitly telling them.

It's okay, even good, if you come across as naïve, imperfect, or wrong. You want to engage the reader with your heartfelt emotions. The more details you reveal about your situation, the more the reader engages with you and becomes your fan.

Rewrite or merge some pages as you continue developing your story line. Use all the writings you've labeled as B in this section, the beginning of your memoir, and create several chapters or essays.

Clear Communication: Only

Your reader needs to know exactly what you mean, so you need to write with exactitude. *Only* is a word that can convey precise meaning if it is in the right place in your sentence. If it is in the wrong place, your reader gets the wrong message.

What do these sentences mean?

1. *James kissed* only *Jenna.*
2. Only *James kissed Jenna.*
3. *James* only *kissed Jenna.*

The first sentence tells us that of all the women at the party James kissed only Jenna.

The second sentence tells us that many men wanted to kiss Jenna, but only James succeeded.

The third sentence tells us that James could have danced with Jenna or chatted with Jenna, but he chose to only kiss her.

Look through your writing and check on your usage of the word *only*.

Day 22

Today you will work on the middle section of your memoir.

Look through all your papers marked M and make sure you have sufficient writings for both internal and external impediments to your quest. Conflict makes your story more interesting and conflicts are caused by obstacles blocking you from achieving your goal. To increase internal blocks, review your patterns (Day 8) and your values (Day 9) and you will remember incidents and ideas that you can write about. A few more pages can be added now.

To increase external blocks consider introducing a person who represents the opposite of what you want. That person adds friction and fear to your situation and then the reader is drawn in and continues reading. Think of a person from your past who could be that external block. Was it someone from work? From your family? Your neighborhood? Perhaps it was a media commentator or newscaster—have you yelled at the radio or television? Add more pages here explaining the oppositional person.

Strong emotion is what your reader wants. Your feelings will be so strong when you write about them, that your reader will feel what you feel. Let your reader know how you experience your passion. Your actions are motivated by your emotions. You can exaggerate and you can write dialogue that the person would probably say, even if you cannot remember exact sentences.

The middle part of your memoir should tell the reader the feelings you have as you attempt to reach your goal. Tell the reader what you must do to surmount the problems blocking you. Allow your reader to know about your fears, your broken heart, your sadness, and your yearnings. Write anecdotes and descriptions for every problem you must overcome and show how you persist. The more action you put into your story the more dramatic and interesting your story is. This is the place to remember all your challenges and dangerous situations. You want the reader to be worried about you.

If you think the middle section of your memoir needs a little more detail, use the questions below to help you:

- How did you accomplish your mission? Build tension by telling your reader what you did to make your quest a reality when it seemed like everything was conspiring against you.

- What happened when you were about to give up? Let your reader know what you felt like when it seemed impossible to succeed.

- What was the crisis that you finally had to confront?

- Did you make a decision? Did you make a difficult choice?

- What had to change? Did you change your plan? Your attitude? Your values? Did you change or modify your goal?

Sample

This is our third trip to Russia. Neither of us has any more vacation days left. We ran out of money on our last trip and my parents are financing this one. This is it. If the bureaucracy won't permit us to go ahead and take Gregory home with us, I might cry my eyes out for weeks, but life will go on. We will donate the crib and the baby bathtub and the stroller and the changing table and the baby clothes, and we will not become parents. It's the saddest day of my life to think we will return to Minneapolis without our baby. His photos are all over our refrigerator and his welcome home party is planned with a caterer and everything. The thought of him continuing to live here, with nothing, no love, no stuff, no good food, nothing at all, is unbearable when we have so much to give him. But I can't get my heart ripped apart again. It's too much for me and it's too much for Mike. Even though he doesn't admit it, I can tell what it's doing to him. So, if they say it's no go, we will leave without the hysterics of last time and without the bribery that didn't do us any good anyway. I remember it all too well. In my dreams every night, Mrs. Z stands with her arms crossed on her chest and says what she said that day, "It's not the right time. You cannot take Gregory yet."

I'm still in Pollyanna mode, so trusting and certain we have a baby that I reply, "Oh, stop kidding around about such a serious matter."

"This is not a joke," Mrs. Z insists.

"Okay. I get it. You want more money from us."

"Yes, more money could be used for the boys. But no travel away this month. Maybe next."

"What? You're serious?"

And that's when I start to shake and scream and carry on like a crazy woman. I think I did go crazy for a few minutes. That won't happen again because Mike and I, if necessary, will go ahead with Plan X. We didn't discuss it with anyone. They'll all be shocked, especially our families. Everyone will find out about it on Facebook. Plan X is the only way we'll be able to live without Baby Gregory. It won't be easy but we'll do it.

The end of your story is near. You're doing a good job. Add stories to this middle section if you think there is more information that the reader should know about your situation.

Clear Communication: Who, Whom

Sometimes it's easy to know whether to use *who* or *whom*. For example, you would not ask, "*Whom* is at the door?", nor would you ask, "*Whom* dropped the book?"

But some sentences are trickier. *Whom/who did you invite to the workshop?*

Here's the trick to get to your answer: Answer that question using both the word *him* and the word *he*. Which sounds best? If it's *him*, then it's *whom*. If it's *he*, then it's *who*. The answer here is *him*, so *whom* is the correct usage. Try it on these sentences:

Who/whom did you go with? You would answer, "*I went with him*," not "*I went with he*," so *whom* is correct.

Who/whom shall I say is calling? He is calling, not *him is calling*, so *who* is correct.

Who/whom do you love? I love him, not *I love he*, so *whom* wins.

Who/whom loves you? He loves you sounds much better than *him loves you*, so the answer is *who*.

Day 23

Today is the day to work on your ending section. This is your grand finale. You will show off to your readers and divulge all the ways in which you have changed.

This is the time to assess your psychological maturity and your spiritual growth. Add to this section by writing about the person you are today. Perhaps you will reveal a universal truth that you were unaware of when you were going through your emotional turmoil. Readers will identify with you as you come to understand more about yourself and about life.

Sample

It took me all these years to appreciate what I had all along. Chasing after the stuff and the women and the money was a game that I was good at, but it didn't do me any good. Maybe you liked reading about my adventures, but in the end all it did was give me a heart condition and too many ex-wives. I have a quiet life now and I am happier than I ever was. My daughter visits—thank God—and has forgiven me. I hope I have many more years like this.

Sample (from Murray)

I'm glad I stuck with the plan and stayed and became a faculty member. It has paid off in many ways. I still can't believe they give me a salary for doing what I love to do. Every day is a joy and I'm happy I didn't quit school all those times when they made it so difficult for me to continue. I treat my students so much better than I ever was treated.

Sample

It's over. I couldn't save him. The doctors couldn't save him. God couldn't save him. I thought I would die, too. But here I am. Not only am I still standing, but yesterday I actually heard myself laugh. Not a big laugh, but a laugh anyway. It seems like I will go on living. But I won't stay here with all the memories. I once had a dream. Then, four years ago when he got so sick, that dream was replaced with the more urgent dream of getting him cured. I never thought I'd survive. But, miracle of miracles, I did even though he didn't. I'm going to try to go back to my original dream. I may be able to pull it off because the fact that I survived these past years tells me I could do anything.

Sample

I still hate when people feel sorry for me, but I don't let it get me depressed like it used to. I go out every day and I do what I have to do. If people stare at me, I don't blame them. It's not every day that you see a person with my type of deformity. Searching out all those doctors and traveling around the country to get all those opinions was worth it. They originally thought I'd be dead years ago. I'm actually proud of who I am and where I am today and I am almost ready to start that foundation for other kids born with my condition.

Even though you cannot change events that happened, you can change the way you interpret those events, even the events that caused you extreme pain. You can end your story with insight, with wisdom, and with maturity.

When you add to the ending of your memoir, please remember to compare yourself now to the way you were when you were just starting your quest and just figuring out what your mission was.

To end your memoir, you will share a lesson or two with your reader. The last pages of your memoir give you the opportunity to clarify everything to the reader, and to yourself, too. This is where you figure out your story and discover parts of yourself you may not have known. Self-examination is welcome here.

Sample

Just because I'm a shrink doesn't mean I know how to choose women. From now on, I am leaving my professional self at the office. I don't want to know anyone's story about childhood abuse or years of mean girls or isolation. I'm done with that. Life is too short to spend it with people I want to fix. I will fix patients at work, but when I am not at work I want Ms. Smiley, or preferably Dr. Smiley. I don't want pathetic people in my home. I don't need to be the healthy one in a sick relationship. I actually do feel healthy when I'm with a mature, healthy person, I think. I've never done that. It's always that they're sick and I'm the healthy fixer. Will I still feel healthy if I'm with a healthy person? I hope so, because starting today I am looking for that gal.

And I can do it. Leaving a bad relationship is a new move for me.

It is ridiculous to be living in the same house with someone whom I'm scared of. I can't pretend it's going to change because in my heart of hearts I know she will always be the way she is now. Even her mother knows how difficult she is. She's been like this for the last couple of years. I have to move on and I have to move out. I need to stop being her shrink. It doesn't matter why she is the way she is. It doesn't matter what caused her to be so full of rage. What matters is that I am living with a woman who is always about to explode at me. I made my decision. I am not understanding her anymore. I refuse to. I am not a psychiatrist. Well, actually I am—but I am not her psychiatrist. I will leave. I will enter new relationships and, eventually, I will find someone who I don't have to understand, but who I can just enjoy without getting involved with her childhood and her wounds. Maybe I just like disturbed people. Well, even if I do I can see them in my office. Never again in my house. I'm done living with disturbed women.

How has your thinking changed? As you reflect upon your life, your struggles, and your successes, think about other people in similar circumstances. Is a universal truth revealed? If you substituted one goal or one idea for another, let your reader know why you did so.

- Did you change your goal because you were defeated?

- Did you find a new way to look at the world?

- Is your new plan a testament to your new maturity?

If your memoir doesn't yet answer the questions above, now is your opportunity to write about these situations to fill out your ending section.

Remember, it's not just what happened; it's what you did with what happened—how you handled it, how it influenced you.

On Day 22 you read about the couple from Minneapolis who were attempting to adopt a baby from Russia. Below is an excerpt from the end of their memoir.

> It's hard to believe that just a few months ago Mike and I felt like our hearts were being ripped out. We still are sad when we think about baby Gregory but there's nothing we can do. The country's rules are firm and he must stay there. We were accepted to the Service Corps and went through the six weeks of training. At the beginning, I hoped we'd have to back out because we would have a baby. But now we're involved deeply with many babies. It's actually an honor and very competitive to get chosen to enter our unit. Everyone here, our supervisors and the families we are helping, appreciates us and all the love that we have to give. I'm sorry for people who desperately want a baby and can't get one, but we are proof that there are other ways to have a good life. Living here, away from the mothers and new babies in their strollers, and away from the conversations about crib mobiles and breast-feeding, helped us. We'll be going back home in two years and I just know we'll be strong.

Is the ending of your memoir amazing? Are you proud of yourself? You are different in many ways than you were at the beginning of your story. The new you is the permanent you, the true you. Your memoir tells your readers that you have come up with a resolution. The resolution is interesting, perhaps even surprising.

Sample

Everybody tells me to stop and smell the roses. I finally figured out that for me it's my work projects that are the roses. I am sorry if no one else loves their job as much as I do, but this is total bliss for me. Smelling roses isn't for everyone. My family thinks that at my age I should give up all the hassles of my job but they don't know that what they consider hassles are challenges for me and I like challenges. No way will I stop.

Sample

Now that you know my story, you know I am not the man everybody thinks of when they see me. You read about my secret hatreds and my cruel thoughts. My life has been an act and it wasn't that hard for me because, as you now know, I am a trained actor. My family was my stage when I was home and not in the theater. I pulled it off and I'm proud of my acting ability.

The people who will be most surprised when they read this memoir will be the people who were taken in by my generosity and charitable contributions. They didn't realize that money doesn't mean that much to me. As long as I didn't have to be pleasant and nice and kind, it was easy to write a check. I pretended for my whole adult life to be a caring person and I smiled and said all the right things, even if I never believed it.

I never liked kids but we had them anyway. I never liked

eating with other people at the table but I did it anyway. I hated baseball but I played with my son. I didn't like our house but I lived in it for all these years. The thing is, I didn't suffer; I just became a phony, but a good phony. I never went to prison and I never hurt anyone and I made a decent family so maybe the mask is the man, after all.

Now that your ending is in place we will use the next days' assignments to expand all your writings and polish your memoir.

Clear Communication: The Colon

A colon (:) tells the reader to slow down and then introduces new information. The information that follows the colon can take the form of a list, a sentence, a quotation, or just a word or phrase. But what precedes the colon must be a complete sentence. Here are a few examples of the correct use of the colon.

> *Judy had one chief goal in her life: to become an American.*
>
> *The following question was asked: Is this the proper use of a colon?*
>
> *Writing offers many benefits: the airing of your soul, a chance for publication, fun with words.*

Note that when the word after the colon begins a new full sentence, that word is capitalized. But when the word is just a sentence fragment it is lower case.

To test if you've used the colon correctly, substitute the word *namely* for the colon. If the sentence still makes sense, you've got it right.

Day 24

Today's assignment is to work on dialogue. It's more interesting to read dialogue than it is to read straight reporting of an incident or conversation.

Consider the following sample:

My dream was to move to a warm climate. I was sick of the New England winters. My obstacle was my husband. He loved our house and our Vermont lifestyle. We were both retired so it wasn't work that kept us in our big old house. It was my husband's stubbornness. One day I decided that we could each have our own way and still be married. I would find an inexpensive apartment to rent for a month in sunny Florida. I did it all over the Internet and then, surprisingly, Charlie agreed to come with me for that month. He knew I was determined to go and he didn't like the idea of having to learn where our kitchen was and how to use the stove. I picked a winner and now we go there every winter for two months. I stood up for what I wanted in a way I never before did. It changed everything.

This could be rewritten, using dialogue, as follows:

My dream was to move to a warm climate. I was sick of the New England winters. My obstacle was my husband.

"Honey, you know I love our house. Why would you want to leave it?"

"These Vermont winters are just too much for me. I can't take the cold anymore."

"That's ridiculous. Winter is the same as it always was."

"But I'm not. I'm going to check out Florida rentals."

I decided that we could each have our own way and still be married. I would find an inexpensive apartment to rent for a month in sunny Florida. I did it all over the Internet.

"Charlie, I got a very good deal and I'll be gone for only one month."

"You're serious, huh? You'd really leave me for all that time?"

"I don't want to leave you, but you don't want to come with me."

"Okay, okay. I don't want you to be by yourself all that time. I'll come down with you. But just this once."

I picked a winner and now we go there every winter for two months. I stood up for what I wanted in a way I never before did. It changed everything.

Dialogue not only makes it more interesting to read, it makes it easier to read, too.

Look back on the essays you've written and locate paragraphs where you described two people speaking but did not use actual dialogue. Change that by rewriting and showing an actual conversation. Whenever a person is speaking, put their words in quotation marks. Have their information come directly from their mouth to the reader.

When you write dialogue, remember that spoken words are often informal short sentences and phrases. In a poorly written dialogue, the conversation might be like this:

"I am so happy Doris is recovering. Dr. Grant says she will be fine."

"I am happy, too. I trust Dr. Grant. He is a good doctor."

"It was very frightening last night. She has a serious disease."

"I agree. I never before felt so frightened."

"I didn't know fever could go up so high."

"I didn't know that, either."

In real life you are more likely to hear conversations like this:

"I'm so happy she's okay."

"Me, too."

"I was scared last night."

"Me, too."

"Did you ever hear of anyone having such a high fever?"

"No, you?"

"Nope."

Read your dialogue aloud and, if it seems stilted and too formal, change some words. (Of course, if it is a formal person who is speaking, then it is appropriate to have stiff language and long sentences.)

As you read all the dialogue you've written in your essays, be sure that the reader knows where the conversation is occurring. Although you may clearly see two people talking while they are sitting at the kitchen table, riding in a car, or waiting in line to get into a movie theater, your reader does not. Your reader needs to be told where your characters are. People do not speak in a vacuum, so describe the background and show the reader everything you visualize when you read those lines of dialogue.

Now that you are a writer, it's a good idea to eavesdrop. Writers are known to sit in coffee shops or on park benches, or to ride on public buses in order to listen to people. Writers want to hear real dialogue spoken by real people. Jot down phrases and use them as a guide when you write dialogue in your memoir. When you recall a line of dialogue you can add more to it as long as it is probably accurate. It need not be a verbatim report. You are not a reporter; you are a storyteller.

While people speak, not only do they say words, they also do something—they push their hair away from their face, crack their knuckles, sip from a water bottle, scrunch their face into a frown, pace the room, and more. When you're out listening to dialogue take notes about the speakers' movements, as well as their words. Your lines of dialogue will be enhanced when you add occasional descriptions of simultaneous motions.

As you look through your writings, you can see the framework of the memoir that you have created. It's okay to move around your writing until you are satisfied that your pieces are in positions that give the reader excellent clarity.

Clear Communication: Me, I

As you write about your relationship with significant people in your life, please know that proper grammar insists that you say, "I am concerned about your mother and *me*," and not, "I am concerned about your mother and *I*."

To help you remember that *me* and not *I* is the correct word add the word *for* before the word you are questioning. You could say, "I am concerned about your mother and *for me*." It would not make sense for you to say, "I am concerned about your mother and for *I*."

Another way to remember is to drop the other person and listen to how it sounds. If you drop *your mother* you would want to say, "I am concerned about *me*." It does not sound acceptable to say, "I am concerned about *I*."

Similarly, when your book is written and you have your book party, you will say, "Please join my family and *me* for a party celebrating the publication of my memoir." It is incorrect to say, "Please join my family and for *I* for a book party."

Day 25

The memoir you have written demonstrates that you have changed. One way to show your reader how you've changed is to reveal what you notice in the world around you.

For example, when you meet someone now perhaps you notice their gleaming teeth or their tailored outfit or their shined shoes or trendy coat. Years past, if you were a flower child, you might have paid attention only to the music they were listening to or the books they were reading. Or maybe you judged people by the car they drove or their job title at work, or maybe their diction and articulation. By mentioning different aspects of your environment and of the people you relate to, you let the reader know what is significant to you.

You might have written about strolling through a particular neighborhood. Walking in downtown Westfield when you are the parent of a small child, you might observe:

> The playground is new, with plenty of climbing structures in primary colors. Parents and some nannies, too, sit on the molded benches and a few toddlers are in the plastic wading pool. I feel welcomed by the enthusiastic cries of the older children as they climb the blue tower.

Walking through the same neighborhood during a time in your life when you are drinking too much, you might notice:

Joe's Bar and Grill is crowded and loud music reverberates from Hank's Hideaway. Where can I go to get a drink and be left alone in quiet misery?

When you are about to buy a new car, every street you pass in downtown Westfield will present you with a dilemma:

Red cars sure look sharp. That silver Subaru looks good, though, and so does that black SUV down near the corner. So many possibilities, so little money.

If you're trying to stick to a diet you'll be charmed by every restaurant:

Vicki's Diner is not crowded. I could just slip right in and get some coffee. The aroma from Bovella's Bakery is so tempting I'm crossing the street. But, oh, there's Sam's Steakhouse.

During times when you are struggling financially, the stores stocked with merchandise will be teasing you:

Look, The Gap is having a sale. And there's a shoe store that has just what I've been looking for.

Please go back to your writings and add some descriptions of people or places based upon what you respected and appreciated at each stage of your personal growth. Add some sentences to pages where you are outdoors. Write about what would capture your attention. Next, find essays you wrote that take place indoors and describe some rooms, paying attention to what you would notice then and now. Wallpaper? Furnishings? Books on the shelves? Scratches on the floor? Windows gleaming or smudged? Your reader wants to see the room in which your action takes place. It's your job to bring that room to life and at the same time give clues about your state of mind, specifically what demands your attention.

Remember to be specific when creating your scenes. If you are talking about a family dinner, it is not sufficient to say, "We all ate too much and now we're going out for a walk." Instead, say, "We stuffed ourselves with turkey, talked with our mouths full, laughed when Cousin Matt did his 'gobble-gobble' routine that he perfected at Thanksgiving, and then we coaxed each other to try to pull ourselves up and take a walk in Claremont Park."

You will surprise your readers when you reveal all aspects of yourself. You are not one-dimensional, and by now they know you well and understand you, too. Take the time to reread all your writing and add sentences and descriptions where appropriate.

Want to add to your memoir? Prompts are phrases that stimulate your thinking and writing. Memoir prompts specifically pry into your past. Below are memoir prompts that may help you remember a long-forgotten incident.

If your mission statement involves your family and familial relationships, then respond to some of these prompts to more fully dramatize your story.

- Why did your parents marry each other?

- When you think of home what words come to mind?

- What celebrations do you remember?

- What was a death that truly mattered?

- How was anger played out in your family?

- What role did religion play in your family?

- What role did divorce play in your family?

If your memoir revisits your childhood, respond to some of these prompts to jog your memory.

- Thinking about your childhood, what do you remember about birthday parties? How did you fare at parties? Were you scared of clowns? Were you shy around the other kids?

- Did you celebrate Halloween? Were costumes a big deal? Did you collect lots of candy?

- What is the best vacation you ever took?

- Did you go to graduation events? Were your accomplishments celebrated? Who was proud of you?

- Are you most comfortable at home or away from home? Were you brave enough to go to sleepovers when you were a child?

Do you need to add more information about your adult life? See the prompts below for ideas:

- What are your most commendable traits today? Did you always think they were commendable? Do others agree?

- Recall a time when you felt betrayed or abandoned. How did you get over it?

- What makes you laugh out loud?

- What is your biggest regret?

- Who is the person you most admire?

- Whose death was the most traumatic for you?

- Who are the people you would like to have for next-door neighbors?

- When you hear the word "home" what memories come to mind?

- If you could have anyone's job, whose would you choose? Why?

- If you had an unlimited amount of money what would you buy for yourself?

- What year of your life do you wish you could repeat?

- Which television personality do you most identify with?

- What role have animals/pets played in your life?

- What's been the most difficult health issue you've had to deal with?

- How has divorce figured in your life?

Keep writing. Your memoir becomes more and more interesting as you add material.

Clear Communication: Passed, Past

You are writing about your *past*, not your *passed*. When you are referring to time the word is *past*. For instance:

> *The orchestra played beautifully in the* past *season.*

When you are referring to action the word is *passed*. For example:

> *When he* passed *the pitcher, the juice spilled.*
> *Very few students* passed *the test this* past *semester.*
> *Within the* past *few minutes, the nurse* passed *the room of the patient who* passed *away.*

Day 26

Today's assignment is to assess the information you've shared with your reader. Is there anything significant that would help the reader understand you and your mission that you've not yet mentioned? Your perspective on life is unique. This is the time to share some of your ideas that might be unusual. Do you have some odd ideas:

- About money?
- About food?
- About medicine?
- About education and schooling?

If you do, and if they are relevant to your mission, please explain these ideas now. Tell your readers how you came to your conclusions. Add this new information to the section of your book where you feel it will be most appropriate.

You also may wish to tell your readers how you have been influenced by:

- Works of art

- Pieces of music—Was music a way to differentiate you from your family?

- Dance experiences

- Movies and films—Were movies an escape for you?

- Television shows

- Theater productions

- Travel experiences

- Lessons and classes

- Sports and team events

- Books and magazines

Sample (from Murray)

I appreciate life and that I am here to live it. I treat my body as a temple and I'm very careful with what I put into it. Of course no alcohol and no cigarettes. But also no sugar and no artificial sweeteners and I try to stay away from processed food. I figure that my body went through so much, I should be good to it now. Fresh fruits and vegetables are my main foods and then eggs and beans when I need protein. I admit it's not easy for me to eat at someone's house. People don't like to invite me to a dinner party, not only because it's difficult to find food for me to eat, but also I make people feel guilty when they are stuffing themselves with junk.

Sample (from Judy)

You might be surprised to know that a person as serious as I am has a most unusual hobby. My hobby is "I Love Lucy." I learned to speak English by watching reruns of that television show. It was on all day and all night. I got to really like Lucy. I have many, many of her shows in my collection and whenever I need a break from some serious scholarly pursuit, I slip a CD into my laptop and watch a Lucy episode. If I'm upset about something, she cheers me up. I wish I could have known her. My husband promised that if we ever have a baby girl we could name her Lucy.

Sample

I made up my mind when I was a young man that I would not chase the dollar. No, I'm not a missionary and I'm not a monk, I'm just a plain guy who lives simply. I don't need the fancy stuff that other people need. Accumulating money doesn't pull me and spending money doesn't pull me. So my life has been based on doing what is interesting even if it pays nothing or very little. My first wife couldn't live like that and my second wife thought she could, but then she couldn't, either. So, now I have another wife and this time I struck pay dirt. She's a pediatrician with enough money on her own. She doesn't mind that I don't like to have stuff and an empty living room doesn't bother her. She calls me Thoreau and is actually proud of me. And I'll tell you about my jobs. I've had more than I can easily count because when I get bored or annoyed I quit. If you don't care about a paycheck, you quit whenever you've had enough. I've worked at a zoo, a hospital, a bookstore, a plumbing shop, a bakery, and many other places, and I had adventures at each place.

This writer's mission statement: *My memoir describes what I went through to live a simple life in the midst of a consumerist society.*

Sample

I saw a movie with Glenn Close and Michael Douglas that totally changed my life. For a bunch of years before I saw that movie, I was divorced and living the life of a woman who loved sex and loved having no attachments. I would pick up men wherever I went because I was in my thirties and single and attractive, if I may say so myself. I would have my way with the guys. I wanted sex and I wanted it two or three times a week and I definitely wanted to go home to my beautiful apartment afterward by myself. I had no desire to share my bed or share anything. If I could have done this without knowing their names, I would have preferred it but most of the guys wanted to talk and get to know me. I had enough friends and a great job. All I needed was sex. I didn't need intimacy or another relationship. It never occurred to me to be worried about these guys. And I never inquired to know if they were married because I didn't care about them. Then I saw the movie.

This writer's mission statement: *My memoir describes what I went through as a single woman trying to survive in Los Angeles.*

Sample

When I was in high school I used to go to Zach's house after dinner and we'd hang out in his backyard or walk into town to the ice-cream shop. One evening, he wasn't finished eating when I came over, and his mom suggested I go and wait with his dad who was down in the rec room listening to music. I said okay and walked down the steps. As I was walking, I heard profound sounds that actually made my heart race. Hal, Zach's dad, was an opera fanatic. I never knew what he did in that basement room every evening and now I knew. He listened to opera. He invited me in and turned up the volume. From that time on, I always left my house early so I could spend an hour listening to opera with Hal. Sometimes we talked and sometimes we just listened to the music. It was the highlight of my day. What would have happened if I didn't go downstairs that day? Maybe I never would have known what opera could do to my soul. My parents did not understand my passion for it. My friends, even Zach, did not. But they all read my columns today and they're proud that I am the opera critic at an important paper.

This writer's mission statement: *My memoir describes how I stumbled into my career.*

Sample

My parents accepted their lot in life and were happy people. They never strived and never tried hard. Every day, they just did what they had to do and then watched television and then they went to sleep. Anything I did was fine with them. They never had expectations for me. So, when I decided to go out for track, they were surprised. They asked me why I wanted to work so hard. They didn't understand competition or striving. If I had not gone to the tryouts that day, I might never have learned the value of hard work and pushing yourself to the limit. Coach's commands are still in my brain and thankfully influence everything I do.

This writer's mission statement: *My memoir describes what I went through to learn to accept my family and respect them for the people they are.*

Please limit your writing to those experiences that are pertinent to your mission.

Carefully decide where in your manuscript to place the additional information about your life that you've just written.

Clear Communication: The Semicolon

This mark of punctuation (;) is one half period and one half comma. So, it's weaker than a period and stronger than a comma.

You use it when you want the reader to slow down but not fully stop. See the sentences below:

> *I never feel bored because I love to read; lucky for me,*
> *there's always an interesting book in the house.*
> *Lucy dashed through the airport; she made the plane.*
> *I like to wash dishes; in fact, I rarely turn on my*
> *dishwasher.*

Day 27

The tone in which you write your essays is significant. Tone is attitude. Your attitude determines your choice of words and tells the reader if you are angry or content, happy or sad, hopeful or impatient, nervous or relaxed.

- Are you looking back on your life with amusement or with disgust?

- Are you serious or frivolous?

- Are you cynical or optimistic?

Your words determine the feeling, the tone, of your writing.

Are you writing a memoir about an illness or surgery? Illness narratives can have serious tones, e.g., "I'm having a mastectomy on Monday", or a lighthearted, flippant tone, e.g., "They're lopping off my breast next week."

In a movie, it is the music that determines the feeling; in a photo, it is the lighting and the shadows; in a painting, it is the color. For you, a writer, words determine what your reader feels and how your reader responds to your writing. If you provide soothing words your reader is relaxed, if you provide angry words your reader is on edge. Different parts of your memoir may have different tones. As you mature, your attitudes change and your writing will reflect that change. Your use of different words, to create different tones, shows the changes throughout your life.

A memoir that begins with this paragraph creates a tone of optimism and affection:

> It was sunny and bright, the boys were on their skateboards and the girls were playing Double Dutch. Mothers were wheeling their babies in carriages and strollers while dads were riding bikes. Music from the outdoor café reached us all the way at the park bench where we were chatting.

The same scene could be depicted in a tone of anxiety and pessimism:

> It was sunny but the kids were not reapplying their sunscreen. The boys were wild on their skateboards, careening into the park fence. Dads were bike riding, but the mothers were saddled with child care. I could barely hear the birds chirping because of noise pollution from that new restaurant.

From a memoir about grandparenting:

> My kids have the audacity to bring up their children their way and not my way.

And from another memoir about being a grandparent:

I worry about the grandchildren. My daughter is much more permissive than I was.

The first memoir will have a humorous and perhaps self-deprecating tongue-in-cheek tone, while the second will be serious and probably judgmental and pedantic.

Your words can create an ominous tone:

My boss shouted at me. My coworker snubbed me. My printer was jammed. This day was not starting very well; I should have stayed home.

Or your words can create a playful tone:

My typical crazy day at the office is beginning. As usual, my boss yells and my coworker stays silent. As usual, my printer decides not to print just when I have something urgent to get out. Welcome to another day in my ridiculous life.

Always be aware of the tone you are creating. You might be tempted to say: *I saw TaylorMae across the room.*

But what did you really mean? What is the tone you wish to convey?

> Did you *glance* at TaylorMae?
>
> *Catch a glimpse* of her?
>
> *Peek* at her?
>
> *Stare* at her?
>
> *Watch* her?

Scrutinize her?

Spot her?

Notice her?

Observe her?

Leer at her?

For today's assignment read all your work and identify the mood and tones in your writing. Then, go back and change some neutral words into words that more strongly express the tones of each section of your memoir.

Clear Communication: The Exclamation Point

It is tempting to end many sentences with this exciting punctuation mark. Do not yield to temptation. When your sentence conveys the idea of excitement by using the appropriate words, the exclamation point is unnecessary. Children tend to use exclamation points because they have limited vocabularies and cannot set the tone of enthusiasm with words. You can do better. Limit the use of exclamation points and give your readers the opportunity to discover zeal and passion by themselves when reading your words. Readers don't need a mark to tell them to feel excited; your words will do that. On the rare occasion when you do use the exclamation mark, please limit it to one such mark after the sentence, not a bunch. One is more than enough!

Day 28

Most of your memoir is now written. You are the main character of your story. You are the protagonist, the hero of your book. Make sure the readers know what you look like, how you think, how you act, and what's important to you. If you've not yet done so, put in descriptions of yourself and also of the other important people in your life. Please look at all your writing and be sure you've described yourself.

You can let the reader know the approximate height of the people you write about by mentioning their height in relation to a stationary object. Your tall dad may look uncharacteristically small next to the giant oak or he may need to duck when he enters the low-ceilinged den. Your petite neighbor may sit on the sofa with her feet dangling because she cannot reach the floor or she may stretch and stand on tiptoe to pull the chain that controls the overhead ceiling fan. You may describe a slight person as looking like a child lost in a large recliner, or a heavy person as someone who causes the sofa to vibrate when he plunks himself down on the middle cushion.

Visual descriptions permit the reader to comprehend and reach conclusions without you stating the obvious. When you describe and show details rather than simply reporting what occurs, you are giving the reader credit for being smart and having the ability to figure out what's going on. Do not overexplain.

Your readers will figure out the age of your characters when you describe the clothing they wear, their hairstyle and hair color, their posture, the music they're listening to, and the slang expressions they use. Think about shoes—would any of your characters wear stiletto heels? Who wears moccasins? Expensive running shoes? Utilitarian sneakers? Shoes reveal something about the person wearing them, and about the trends during the particular years in which your memoir takes place. Please go back to your writing and add details about clothing.

You can reveal the approximate age of your characters without explicitly stating a number by alluding to certain characteristics. Younger people tend to carry themselves more erectly than do elderly folks—the latter may have stooped shoulders. Gray hair and sensible shoes usually belong to the older folks, too. The technique of showing and not explicitly telling ages is illustrated in the sentences below:

> It seemed like she was contemplating her retirement even though she was giving me career advice.
>
> High school students are much different nowadays. Back when I was his age . . .
>
> When he got out of the car, he reminded me of my grandpa.
>
> As typical worried new parents, we consulted advice books every day.
>
> I smiled and wondered if she realized she had one pair of glasses hanging around her neck and another on top of her head.
>
> You'd never know he's a new driver.

Now is the time to examine descriptions. Whenever you mention a person, any person, be sure the reader knows how that person fits into your life and not only what that person looks like and their approximate age, but their style. Every character about whom you write has a unique style, an individual way of speaking, of walking, of relating to others. Differentiate your characters.

Personality can be revealed by speaking habits. For example, indicate that someone is domineering by showing how that person interrupts, speaks loudly, or finishes others' sentences. And then there's the timid person who looks at his shoes while speaking and mostly mumbles. The show-off may use huge vocabulary words and may wildly gesticulate.

Next, find ways to show the reader every person's mood. Are your characters wearing dull gray or bright yellow? Are they walking with a bounce or a shuffle? Are they sitting slouched or upright? Do they answer questions with one-word answers? Do they avoid making eye contact? Can they barely sit still because they are so filled with enthusiasm? Add these important enhancers to your essays.

When you talk about a feeling, describe the accompanying physical response. Do you tremble when you're frightened? Blink when you feel stressed? Blush when embarrassed? What feeling makes your heart race? Under what circumstances do you sigh? What gives you a headache? When you mention an emotion, let the reader know what that emotion does to you and to the people you are writing about.

When you portray a character, don't simply use a word to describe a characteristic but instead illustrate the characteristic. Instead of saying that Tommy was a pest because he pulled pranks, say, "Oh, here he goes again, that Tommy, now he's hiding Mom's keys in the freezer and when she goes looking for them he'll finally find them and tell her that she's losing it." Each person you write about should have a distinguishing habit or style.

Do some of your essays take place in the kitchen? Is food a significant part of your life and your family's interaction? You can show style by describing a dinner table. Are folks drinking from beer cans or sipping white wine? Is there fine china on a tablecloth or are there paper plates on dad's lap while he watches TV? Instead of saying that Uncle Harry is dull, show him eating a plain frank on a roll every night. Instead of saying that Aunt Linda is sophisticated, show her pouring Gorgonzola vinaigrette on her salad. Is there white bread on the table or is the bread an artisanal wholegrain loaf? Check all your writing and insert specific foods where appropriate.

Inspect your entire memoir for people and the ways in which you've presented them. Rewrite where necessary. Each person should be depicted so well and so thoroughly that if any character in your memoir suddenly showed up in real life, every reader would know who it was.

Your characters are real to you and you can see them in your mind. Your mandate is to allow your readers to see them, too. Please thoroughly check every page you have written. Now is the time to add more description and thereby enhance your memoir.

Clear Communication: Parallel Structure

Do you notice anything awkward in the sentence below?

You are writing rapidly, efficiently, and in a competent way.
Read it aloud and you will hear a good rhythm at the beginning of the sentence but an unwieldy ending. Now read this sentence:

You are writing rapidly, efficiently, and competently.

Each of the words in the lists ends in *ly,* so the sentence sounds much better. Each of those words has a structure that is parallel to the others; hence, there is parallel structure.

Which of these sentences sounds best to you?

> *Peter enjoys hiking, biking, and going swimming.*
> *Peter enjoys hiking, biking, and swimming.*

The second version is correct because each of the words in the list consists of just one word. No need for the word *going.*

The words or phrases in a list should be similar (parallel) in grammatical form and in length. In the sentences that follow, the first version is clumsy, the second is correct.

> *1. Writing a memoir is stimulating and creates a challenge.*
> *2. Writing a memoir is stimulating and challenging.*

> *1. I do my best gardening in April, May, and in June.*
> *2. I do my best gardening in April, May, and June.*

> *1. I like to read, writing, and thinking.*
> *2. I like reading, writing, and thinking.*

> *1. To graduate, Joseph needs a letter from his teacher, a list of books read, and they also want to know his plans for next year.*
> *2. To graduate, Joseph needs a letter from his teacher, a list of books read, and a written statement of his plans for next year.*

Please check your memoir to be sure you have used parallel structure and have similar patterns to the words in your lists.

Day 29

Your memoir does not take place in a blank space. It's necessary to create scenes. One way to create a scene is by describing places and events in great detail, with specificity. Tomorrow's assignment will explain another way to create a scene, by adding action to the details.

Read the two statements below.

> 1. *I remember the day that I first met Susan. It was love at first sight.*

> 2. *It was on a rainy Sunday in April that I first met Susan. I couldn't take my eyes off her—those dimples were compelling.*

Which sounds better? Which brings you into the situation? Which provokes more feelings in you? Which contains a cliché? The second sentence helps you visualize the scene. The writer described Susan's dimples, and then let the reader know the season, the day of the week, and the weather. Those facts help the reader see the scene. Please put into words whatever it is you are seeing in your mind when you write your sentences.

It is important to create a scene your reader can visualize. For example, instead of stating:

Soon I will graduate from high school, leave this suburban community, and get to New York City.

you might say:

The calendar on my bedroom wall reassures me that in just 11 more days I'll be on my way to the next chapter of my life. I can practically hear the subway sounds and see the yellow taxis and the throngs of people.

Note that the latter sentence does not mention the name of the city, but the reader infers it.

In the next example, instead of stating:

My tour of duty is almost finished and I can't wait to get home and propose to Emily.

you might say:

Emily's silky blond hair and beautiful blue eyes help me get through these last few weeks here on base and I've already emailed Hank's Jewelry Shop in town. She'll be so surprised.

The second sentence does not use the term engagement ring but the reader will figure it out.

In the first example above, the reader wonders if the author is prepared to succeed in a big city. In the second example, the reader is curious to know if the writer will arrive home safely and if Emily will say yes to the marriage proposal. The more opportunity you give to the reader to make inferences, the more that reader participates in your scene and becomes your supporter.

Read the two sentences below:

> 1. *It's sunny, the garden is beautiful today and that makes me feel happy.*
>
> 2. *The daffodils are shining in the sunlight, the bees are busily working in the garden, and the one white cloud that's drifting across the blue sky seems to be smiling at me.*

The first example reports in general terms; the second creates a scene.

The more specificity you use, the more the reader is brought into the scene. Hooking your reader is your goal. You don't want a reader who is disinterested or bored because that's the reader who easily puts down your book in favor of another.

Instead of:

It was a windy day

you might try:

Leaves swirled through the streets, women clutched their scarves, children hung on to their parents' coats, and tree limbs threatened every passerby.

Notice that the wind is not mentioned in the second sentence but the reader easily realizes it's a windy day.

Below are five sentences that you can practice on. Come up with an expanded sentence—or two—to give your reader a clearer picture of the scene. I've participated in this, too, so you can see the sentence(s) I came up with after you write your version.

1. *I am so happy.*

2. *I prefer the city to rural life.*

3. *These new shoes are killing me.*

4. *The kids ran downstairs. They were glad to see my brother.*

5. *The house was a mess. There were so many things on the floor.*

Here are my expanded descriptions:

1. *My smile is wide and my heart is hopeful.* (Try not to mention happiness in your sentence.)

2. *I'm settling down to read this month's* National Geographic. *It's what I do on those rare occasions when I become afflicted with an urge for the out-of-doors.* (I used humor and exaggeration for this one.)

3. *My heel is bleeding, my little toe probably fell off two blocks ago, and, after every step I take, I expect flames to come shooting out from under my feet.* (More exaggeration.)

4. *Amy and Jed flew down the steps and barraged Uncle Tim with high fives and hugs.* (I mentioned names and showed action to make the scene more real.)

5. *The floor was littered with soda cans, beer bottles, and discarded baby diapers.* (I gave a visual description and I used some words to arouse interest.)

There is no right answer; your reader will see whatever you have described. Remember that book readers are not mind readers. They do not know what you are visualizing when you write your scenes. Only your words can make it clear to them. Use specific details to help each reader get the same picture in their head that you already have. The more specific every sentence is, the better written your memoir is. Embellish your scenes with distinctive details.

You are a writer; you are not a summarizer. Please read all your pages now and check to see if the reader is presented with a picture of the setting of your story. Search for sentences you can expand by pretending you are the reader and you know nothing about the people or places that you are reading about. Add the appropriate words to create the appropriate images.

Be specific. The sentences below illustrate that it's always better to use one exact word rather than a few more general words.

He ran quickly could be replaced by *He raced.*

She is very smart could be replaced by *She is brilliant.*

The author wrote too little description could be replaced by *The author wrote scant description.*

The room didn't have a lot of furniture in it could be replaced by *The room was sparsely furnished.*

I hope you do very well could be replaced by *I hope you flourish.*

There is too much traffic could be replaced by *The roads are clogged.*

As you read all the pages of your memoir and look for words and phrases that you can improve upon, have a thesaurus handy. There is a thesaurus that is part of your word-processing program and it can be up on your screen at all times. Use precise words. Author Catherine Drinker Bowen has said, "For your born writer, nothing is so healing as the realization that he has come upon the right word." When you use words that are exact, you distinguish your memoir from amateur stories.

Clear Communication: Italics, not Quotes

Do you want to emphasize certain words? Do not put those words inside quotation marks. If you must draw attention to a word, put that word in italics. Do not, do not use quotation marks. Here are some examples of what not to do:

> *"Ripe" bananas on sale*
> *Dog "lost" on Fifth Street*
> *Breakfast served "now."*

These are actual signs placed on store windows.

Day 30

Congratulations! You're almost finished with your memoir. The remaining task is to improve your scenes by adding action. We'll begin by investigating the examples below:

1. *We all saw Rosie cheating at our card game. Ellen confronted her, so then Rosie ran out.*

2. *The four of us were in the senior center playing 500 rummy. Rosie sat up straight, very straight, so straight and tall that she could glance down and see all of Ellen's cards.*
   "Cut that out," Ellen warned.
   Rosie feigned innocence. She tried to look confused, but within minutes, she picked up her glasses, her purse, and her sweater and bolted out the door.

The author created a scene in the second example, while the first was just a summary. Although their ages were never stated, in the second example, the reader knows the approximate age of the women because the writer provided clues: senior center, glasses, sweater. The author has created a true action scene.

Action scenes have:

1. A beginning action (Rosie glancing at Ellen's cards)

2. A strong feeling or conflict that emerges (Ellen telling her to stop)

3. An opposing action, or reaction, that occurs (Rosie running out)

Below, you can again see the difference between a summary and a scene (at this juncture it is not yet an action scene).

1. *Her boyfriend came into the house and made himself at home, as if nothing had happened.*

2. *Clark walked through the sitting room, ignored the housekeeper, and marched into the living room, uninvited. He plopped himself into the black leather recliner, pushed back, and put his feet up, and with a smirk, tried to join our conversation.*

The first sentence is a summary; the second example is a scene.

Below is an excerpt from a memoir about the author's relationship with Mary, her adult daughter, who has a serious chronic disease. The author lets us know the socioeconomic status by mentioning the sitting room, the housekeeper, and the leather recliner. Find ways in your writing where you can specify items to communicate values and status.

Read how the memoirist expands the above scene to create an action scene:

Clark walked through the sitting room, ignored the housekeeper, and marched into the living room, uninvited. He plopped himself into the black leather recliner, pushed back and put his feet up, and with a smirk, joined our lively conversation.

I didn't invite him into my house and I don't want him here. But Mary is my houseguest for the next few days so I have to be polite to him. Maybe I'll be lucky and they'll break up today. Their fights are getting longer and louder.

Mary is having a good day today. Her coloring is good and she has stamina. Sometimes she looks her age but other times she looks like an old lady, even older than I am. The medications do damage to her skin and her nails. Her hair is starting to show some strands of gray but she still has a good figure.

Clark is looking at her with love and that makes me feel good for a moment, and a little bit guilty that I want to get rid of him. But then I remember what he's really like and what he has said and what he has done. I can't let myself be fooled by him . . . again. I'm her mother and I must protect her. I've got to get him to show his true colors.

"Clark, I heard your building had some vandalism. What was that about?" I ask.

"Nobody knows why a guy would want to smash those mirrors in the lobby, ya know," Clark said.

"The police report in the paper said it was a tenant who was very angry and had a fight with the landlord."

"Whadda the cops know?"

"Well, they did do an investigation."

Mary starts to fidget. "Ma, that's all over. Just drop it."

Analyzing the above scene, we first see that something happened—Clark arrives unexpectedly. Then we see the writer's conflict, which is between wanting her daughter to be happy with her boyfriend and believing that the boyfriend is bad news. Then the writer takes action, deciding to bait him in the hope he will reveal his true character.

When you read through your memoir, expand your scenes so you have something close to this sequence: a beginning action, the emergence of a strong feeling or conflict, and then a reaction or opposing action.

Each scene you write needs to have something happen, something change. Once the change occurs, your conflict, trouble, or dilemma is apparent. Your feelings are intense and you make a decision that results in an action.

Readers don't have patience to read pages of nothing happening, no matter how lovely your writing is and how pretty your descriptions are. They want movement. The actions and reactions that occur in your writings don't necessarily have to involve physical movement; they can be emotional or psychological changes.

Today's assignment is to expand your scenes. Examine your sentences and choose a few to rewrite so that you create a scene, a visual representation that your reader can connect to. And while you are reading your pages please be brave enough to "kill the darlings." This is a writer's term that means if while reading your work you realize a particular sentence or word or phrase is not appropriate for your story you will remove it—even if it is clever, even if you love the way it sounds, even if it is a "darling."

Life holds every possibility, from peril to glory, from risk to triumph. No matter what occurs, life persists and you have lived to tell the tale. Tell it with enthusiasm. You are the expert on your life. Write with authority and let the world know your story. But don't rush. Make certain your memoir is as good as it can be before you consider publishing it. Please read every page you have written and take the time to revise and enhance your sentences.

And then . . . you're done! You have written your memoir. Excellent work! I look forward to reading your story; email it to me after you have "workshopped" it and rewritten it at least once or twice. See the appendix on the next page for more information on your publishing path. You can reach me through my website, memoirclassonline.com. Good luck!

Appendix

Your Publishing Path

Prepublication

Authors "workshop" their writing before they submit it for publication. "Workshopping" means reading it to a group of other writers and asking each member of the group for feedback. Writers' workshops abound; they are at public libraries and bookstores, and online, too. Put the words memoir and workshop into a search engine and you'll have many workshopping opportunities to choose from. Add the name of your city and you'll meet neighbors who are also writing memoirs. There are annual conventions and conferences in cities throughout the world for writers in general, and memoir writers in particular.

Feedback should have two components—the story and the writing. Some memoirists have a terrific story to tell but need help with grammar and word choice. Others are excellent writers but tell a story that is too scattered, and the plot or narrative arc is underdeveloped. Your memoir will be ready for publication when both the writing and the story are deemed excellent.

The usual route to publication consists of:

1. Writing

2. Editing by an editor

3. Rewriting

4. Workshopping

5. Rewriting

6. Workshopping again

7. Rewriting

8. Self-publishing or locating a literary agent who will represent you to a publisher

It's a good idea to compile a list of possible conferences or workshops to attend, and editors or book doctors to interview. There are several excellent writers' magazines that list all upcoming workshops and conferences for aspiring writers.

While most writers enjoy workshops, some find it annoying to listen to other members of the group read their writings. If you fall into that latter category and prefer a one-on-one experience, you can always pay an editor, a memoirist, or a book doctor to read and critique your memoir. A book doctor is an experienced author/ editor who helps you polish your manuscript and get it ready for publication. The book doctor is your shepherd who accompanies you and your book to your publishing goal. Be sure to negotiate payment in advance. Some book doctors charge by the hour, others by the project. Your book doctor will help you identify what needs to be fixed and then will show you how to fix it or send you to the appropriate person to fix it, or perhaps even fix it for you.

Also, now is the time to decide who will be your first reader. Certainly all your loved ones are eager to read your memoir. But will they give you honest critiques?

Choose someone who is not related to you and not a very close friend. You want a reader who is intelligent enough to appreciate what you've written and also brave enough to be a stern critic when necessary.

Memoirists often begin their publishing career by sending one essay to a newspaper or a magazine that regularly publishes such essays. Go to a large newsstand or bookstore, look through the newspapers and the magazines and note which ones accept memoir excerpts. Carefully examine the published memoir essays that you find and then replicate the format when you submit yours—word count is most important, but also notice whether they prefer humorous or serious essays, essays about childhood or adulthood, essays about family dilemmas or worldwide situations. In addition to the magazines and newspapers, there are a plethora of online sites that accept memoir essays. Seek and ye shall find.

Whether you submit online or in print, to a newspaper or a magazine, track down the guidelines for each publication by putting the word *guidelines* into a search engine along with the name of the magazine or newspaper. Guidelines specify the particular requirements of each publication. For example, some magazines or newspapers will not accept a submission if you are sending it to other publications, too. Their guidelines will indicate that they accept only exclusive submissions and not simultaneous submissions. Guidelines will inform you of particular themes and subjects that are of interest, and will tell you about word count and whether or not you can expect payment if your piece is published.

If you are a perfectionist and must write and rewrite several times, that's just fine. In fact, that's the recommended way to proceed toward publication. If you are an extreme perfectionist and must write and rewrite for years and years, figure out why you are reluctant to finish your manuscript. Sometimes, perfectionism is based upon the erroneous idea that everyone is interested in what you are saying, eager to criticize you, enthused about judging you, and waiting to pounce. That's simply not true. No one will read your memoir as thoroughly as you will. Readers just want to read a good story; they're not interested in examining the author.

Do not permit fear of failure to prevent you from getting your story out—whether to the public, to family and friends, or just for yourself. Instead of thinking about yourself and how you are coming across, think about your readers and their desire for a good book. If you've rewritten and workshopped and perhaps rewritten again, you're ready to publish. Go for it!

Self-Publishing

Transforming your thoughts, your feelings, and your raw emotions from memories into a narrative is the creative part of producing your memoir. There are other parts crucial to making your memoir a book—the business tasks.

Your first order of business is to decide who your readers will be.

- Is your memoir for only your family and closest friends?

- Is it for business colleagues?

- Did you write it for the world at large?

- Are you hoping to become a *New York Times* best-selling author?

- Did you write for a certain group of people who share a specific interest?

If you are writing for family, friends, or a limited number of colleagues you can self-publish your memoir. Simply go to your local copy shop and print and bind each book or booklet.

If you wish to self-publish with the goal of selling your book to a wider audience—not just family and friends—your book will need all the professional touches of a bookstore book. So, you will need to do the work that a traditional publisher would ordinarily do for you, or hire a self-publishing company to do those jobs. Such work includes:

- Editing and proofreading

- Obtaining an ISBN number—that's the unique thirteen-digit number that will identify your book

- Registering for a Library of Congress copyright

- Formatting the pages with appropriate typefaces, fonts, graphics, headers and footers, and margins

- Writing what is called the front matter—those are the first pages that have roman numerals (i, ii, iii, iv, v, and so on). They include the title page, copyright information, dedication page, table of contents, preface, and introduction

- Designing the front and back covers

- Binding, choosing paper, and printing

- Marketing the book

- Storing the book in your home

- Figuring out how to get orders from bookstores and individual readers

- Processing the payments and establishing a bookkeeping system

- Packaging and mailing the books

- Negotiating subsidiary rights—including book clubs, paperback reprints, and much more

If your readership is to extend beyond your loved ones you will need to:

- Develop a website

- Organize a direct mail campaign

- Create chat rooms

- Compile email lists of potential readers

- Talk to local bookstore owners

- Ask people you know, and many you don't know, for laudatory blurbs you can put on your book cover

- Identify critics who will review your book in magazines, newspapers, and online

- Arrange to promote your book on radio and television and perhaps in magazine ads, too

This is all part of the business of getting people to buy copies of your memoir.

When you self-publish, you decide what to charge for your

book and you keep all the money that you earn, whereas a traditional publisher pays you a royalty that is a small percentage, usually between 10 and 15 percent, of the price of the book. That's the good news about self-publishing. The other good news is that you can write your book the way you want without having to make changes that traditional publishers often demand. Nor do you have to go through the efforts, which are many, to attract a traditional publisher.

A number of companies now offer services that help you accomplish some of these tasks. Check the Internet to familiarize yourself with all your options for self-publishing. For instance, the publisher of this book, Reader's Digest, has partnered with Author Solutions, Inc. to form LifeRich Publishing, a company that will help you convert your manuscript into a book that anyone can buy either in a bookstore or online. Your book can be available as a hardcover, paperback, or e-book.

Traditional Publishing

To interest a traditional commercial book publisher in your memoir, you usually need to go through an intermediary called a literary agent, although a few publishers do accept books without representation from an agent.

How do you get an agent? It's not easy. You must spark their interest in your memoir. Your first task, if you want a publisher or an agent to read your manuscript, is to send them a query letter. A query letter is just one page on which you summarize the story you have written, introduce yourself, and explain why you are qualified to write that story, and then suggest who your reader, also called your audience, would be. Of course we all want our readers to be everyone, everywhere, but you will need to be more specific. Does your book hold more interest for a woman? A married person? An elderly person? An outdoorsman? A person going through a life-changing trauma? You get the idea. You must identify your audience.

There are books and magazines for writers that list agents and publishers and the types of writing that interests them, along with their contact information. You also may want to spend a day at a bookstore, locate the memoir section, and look through many memoirs. Identify some memoirs that are similar in style or content to yours and then search for the Acknowledgement section. Usually, acknowledgements are in the front of the book, but sometimes at the end. This is the page on which the author names those who have been helpful during the writing and publishing process. Take note of the names of agents and editors, ignore the praises offered to spouses and neighbors. You now have names of publishing professionals you can contact because you know that they appreciate your type of writing.

If your query letter, which may be in email form, intrigues the publisher or agent you will then be asked to submit a book proposal. The book proposal is a big deal. It is a summary of the book you have written, including an excerpt, plus much more. The proposal must include information about competing books and about your platform.

Competing books are already published and somewhat similar to your proposed book. The publisher wants to know that your book is not about a topic so obscure that no one will ever buy it; and if there are books similar how are they doing—are they selling well or are they languishing on the shelves? And how is your book different and better than those already published? So, you'll need to spend a day or two at a bookstore and online doing research about comparable books.

An author needs a platform and as a prospective author, you

must develop your platform. A platform is the compilation of all the ways in which you can communicate with your readers. You may communicate through Twitter and Facebook, or perhaps through a newspaper or magazine column that you write. Maybe you'll use your blog, your website, the classroom where you teach, the organizations for which you do volunteer work, or any public-speaking opportunities that come your way to communicate with your readers. Online interaction is an important part of your platform and your prospective agent or publisher wants to see a strong Google presence. The time to develop your platform is today. The larger your platform, the more likely a literary agent or a publisher will be interested. Once your book comes out, the larger your platform, the larger your sales will be. Publishers are investing money in you and want you to prove that you have a following of people who know about you and are interested in what you have to say.

Prepare your manuscript according to professional standards by using Times New Roman 12 or 14 as your font, or another clean, readable font, and by numbering your pages. Do not use any fancy fonts or any elaborate adornments. The first page should have only the title and your name and email address and phone number if you submit by email. If you submit by snail mail, include your street address, too. Please double space your manuscript and write only on one side of each paper. Some agents and publishers prefer no bindings, no stapling, just pages, so ask about preferences before you submit.

Although this may seem intimidating, there are many books and online sites that carefully teach you, step-by-step, how to appeal to a literary agent, write a dynamic query letter, and prepare a comprehensive book proposal.

You can do all this. You will do all this. And it's definitely worth it.

Marketing and Sales

If you are distributing your memoir to a limited number of readers (your family, for instance, or your employees), you don't need to be concerned with marketing and sales. But if you want to reach a wider audience, your work has just begun. Your book will languish on a bookstore shelf unless you contact people to inform them that the book exists and then persuade them to buy it.

Many years ago, when my first book was published, the publisher flew me first-class on a nationwide tour and put me up at five-star hotels. They booked me on major radio and television shows, and newspaper reporters came to my hotel at each city to interview me. Times have changed. With my last few books, the publishers smiled sweetly and reiterated that their very small publicity departments were devoted to their celebrity authors. They wished me well and hoped I could create visibility for myself. (I was fortunate because I was already a published author. If I were not, I would have had to establish my platform before the publisher would even agree to publish my book.) It was my job to get publicity, arrange speaking engagements, and ensure that my book would appear when a prospective reader went to a search engine for a topic I wrote about.

Whether you work with a traditional publisher, choose to go with a helpful self-publishing company, or do it entirely on your own, you will need to find ways to market your book. Once again, the Internet is your friend. Searching online, you can find free advice about marketing your memoir. You can also locate public relations companies that specialize in book marketing, if you choose to hire one. You will need to send emails, as well as tweets, Facebook announcements, Instagram photos, and other social media communications to everyone you know, and to many whom you do not know. The more you spread the word, the more your book will sell. Put energy and time, money if you have it, into helping your memoir become a good seller. It's worth your effort.